Alaskan Klee Kai

Ultimate Care Guide

Includes: Alaskan Klee Kai Training, Grooming, Lifespan, Puppies, Sizes, Socialization, Personality, Temperament, Rescue & Adoption, Shedding, Breeders, and More

Dr Margaret Shepperton

Copyright © 2023 by Dr Margaret Shepperton

No part of this book may be reproduced, stored in retrieval systems, or transmitted by any means, electronic, mechanical, photocopying, recorded or otherwise without written permission from the author or publisher.

Acknowledgements

With grateful thanks to the many Alaskan Klee Kai lovers out there who own or would like to own this wonderful dog. Without you this book could not have gone from being an idea, to becoming a formal book. You're a true inspiration. Thank You.

There are times in life when you come across unique individuals who are full of love and selfless in their nature.

Pamela and Ken Renfrew - I would like to take this opportunity to thank you both for your kind support during this journey. It will always be remembered.

Lisa Chapman – it was a great pleasure to work with you. Thank you for donating your amazing photography skills.

Cendrine Huemer – Thank You for your wonderful support. Your finely crafted editing skills and contributions were very much appreciated.

Table of Contents

CHAPTER 1: INTRODUCTION 4

CHAPTER 2: UNDERSTANDING ALASKAN KLEE KAI 7

CHAPTER 3: THE PERSONALITY OF THE ALASKAN KLEE KAI .17

CHAPTER 4: FINDING A KLEE KAI 21

CHAPTER 5: GETTING READY FOR PUPPY 31

CHAPTER 6: BRINGING PUPPY HOME 45

CHAPTER 7: CARING FOR YOUR ALASKAN KLEE KAI 57

CHAPTER 8: FEEDING YOUR ALASKAN KLEE KAI 79

CHAPTER 9: SOCIALIZING AND TRAINING YOUR ALASKAN KLEE KAI 95

CHAPTER 10: ALASKAN KLEE KAI HEALTH 107

CHAPTER 11: BREEDING YOUR ALASKAN KLEE KAI 137

CHAPTER 12: COMMON TERMS 164

CHAPTER 13: RESOURCES 188

Chapter 1: Introduction

Chapter One: Introduction

The Alaskan Klee Kai is a small breed of dog with beautiful, husky-like coloring in a small package. However, despite their size, the Alaskan Klee Kai is a dog with a huge personality.

And I mean huge. Anyone who has ever owned an Alaskan Klee Kai has quickly fallen in love with their good natured temperament. They are intelligent, energetic and athletic but they are also a breed that also loves to be with their people.

With all these amazing qualities, it really is quite amazing that the Alaskan Klee Kai is not in the top 10 most popular breeds.

What is even more amazing is the lack of information out there about the Alaskan Klee Kai. Many people are unaware of the breed and there is little out there to introduce them.

For those who have the honor of owning an Alaskan Klee Kai, it can be very frustrating since there is little out there for owners. But that is about to change with this book.

I love Alaskan Klee Kai and I know, first hand, how difficult it is to gather the information needed to care for them. That is the reason that I wrote this book -- to show everyone how wonderful the breed truly is.

In addition, I will go over the history of the breed, what it should look like and the temperament you can expect from your Alaskan Klee Kai puppy.

But I do not stop with just the breed profile, I go over the needs of the Alaskan Klee Kai breed, the care that you should give your puppy and dog and also how to feed your pup.

Chapter One: Introduction

I take you through common health problems the Alaskan Klee Kai breed faces and how to choose a puppy to help minimize the risks of these diseases.

Finally, I take you through breeding the Alaskan Klee Kai and producing healthy and happy puppies.

By the time you are done reading this book, you will realize how wonderful the Alaskan Klee Kai is and how amazing it is to share a life with one.

Chapter 2: Understanding Alaskan Klee Kai

Chapter Two: Understanding Alaskan Klee Kai

As with any animal, one thing that I recommend everyone do before they purchase the animal is to learn as much about the animal as possible. This is extremely important when it comes to owning a dog. The main reason is because dogs come in hundreds of different sizes, temperaments and breeds and this can affect the overall needs of the individual dogs.

While a dog may look cute, some breeds do not fit with some people. Breeds that are always on the go are not recommended for people with limited mobility while a lazy breed isn't recommended for people who are active. Knowing the breed's traits before you bring home a puppy will ensure that the puppy is the right fit for you.

Which brings us to the Alaskan Klee Kai. This small and active little breed is quickly gaining popularity but there is a lot that every owner should know about the breed before they make their purchase.

This chapter is designed just for that and I will take you through the history of the Alaskan Klee Kai, the breed standard and finally some general facts about the breed.

1. What is an Alaskan Klee Kai

The Alaskan Klee Kai is a small sized breed of dog that is a loyal little dog with a big heart and a unique temperament.

It is a spitz type dog that was created in the United States, or more specifically in Alaska as an alternative to the Alaskan Husky. The breed was developed to be the apartment-sized Alaskan Husky.

Chapter Two: Understanding Alaskan Klee Kai

2. History of the Alaskan Klee Kai

As I mentioned, the Alaskan Klee Kai was developed in Alaska, USA as an alternative to the Alaskan Husky. The breed owes its creation to a woman by the name of Linda Spurlin.

During the 1970's, Linda Spurlin came into possession of a small Siberian Husky cross. From that puppy, she realized how wonderful the breed was and began her breeding program of smaller huskies.

While it is unclear what breeds went into the original Siberian Husky cross, Linda Spurlin put great thought into the development of the breed and decided to add more Siberian Huskies when she was creating the Alaskan Klee Kai.

Although the breed was developed in the 1970s, she kept the breed to herself and her family. None of her dogs were sold and the breeding program was focused on selecting

Chapter Two: Understanding Alaskan Klee Kai

the best dogs that conformed to the look and temperament that she wanted.

However, in 1988, the Spurlin family opened up their kennel for new owners. Originally calling the breed the Klee Kai, it was quickly changed to the Alaskan Klee Kai in 1995.

Breeders today strive to maintain the integrity of the breed and are working towards recognition with kennel clubs around the world. The Alaskan Klee Kai was accepted by the United Kennel Club (UKC) in 1997 and has continued to gain popularity as more people learn about this wonderful breed.

3. Breed Standard of the Alaskan Klee Kai

As with all breeds, the Alaskan Klee Kai has a breed standard. This means that there is a set temperament, look, coloring and size of the breed that the dogs should conform to.

The Alaskan Klee Kai is a small breed of dog that should look very similar to an Alaskan Husky, only smaller. The overall build of the dog should be one of an athletic and quick dog with a slightly rectangular shape. The length of the Alaskan Klee Kai should be slightly longer than they are tall.

The head of the Alaskan Klee Kai should be wedge-shaped with a slightly rounded skull. There should be a clean look to the head with a moderate stop at the muzzle. The muzzle itself should be slightly shorter than the skull and should have a taper to it.

Chapter Two: Understanding Alaskan Klee Kai

The nose of the Alaskan Klee Kai should be black, but a snow nose, which is pink streaked, or liver colored nose on a red and white coat is acceptable.

Teeth should come together in a scissor bite while the lips of the Alaskan Klee Kai should be black, with the exception of liver in red and white dogs. A level bite, undershot, overshot or wry mouth is not acceptable.

The eyes of the Alaskan Klee Kai should be almond shaped and should be medium in size. They can be found in a range of colors including blue and can also have eyes that are different colors.

The ears of the Alaskan Klee Kai should be medium in size, although they will look slightly large in comparison to the head. They should be triangular in shape and should stand straight up and pointed forward.

Alaskan Klee Kai have a medium length neck that is slightly arched. The breed should have a body that is sloping slightly, with the shoulders higher than the rump. Ribs should be well sprung and the spine should be strong.

The tail of the Alaskan Klee Kai should be high on the dog and should have a loose curl to it. This curl can cover over the back or drape to either side of the body. It should be well furred.

Overall, the Alaskan Klee Kai should have the size and shape of a small breed but the overall build of an athletic dog.

a) Coloring

Alaskan Klee Kai can be found in a variety of patterns, with only three distinct colors. These are red and white,

Chapter Two: Understanding Alaskan Klee Kai

black and white and grey and white. Completely white Alaskan Klee Kai can also be found but are not desired in show quality dogs.

Despite having only three colors, the Alaskan Klee Kai is a varied breed with a range of coat patterns. The mask should extend down the muzzle, under the eyes and over the skull. The dog should have a facial mask that is clearly visible.

In addition to the mask, the dog's throat, breeches, chest, legs, paws and underside should be a lighter shade or white. There can be other markings on the dog but the dog should have a look of symmetry.

b) Coat

The Alaskan Klee Kai coat should consist of a thick undercoat that is soft and should cover the dog completely. It should have a sufficient length where you can see the undercoat. One thing to note is that during shedding periods of the year, the Alaskan Klee Kai can lose their undercoat.

Chapter Two: Understanding Alaskan Klee Kai

The topcoat should be longer than the undercoat, and coat length varies in the breed. Some have a medium length coat and others have a longer one. These coat types are actually split into two coat varieties; the standard, which is the shorter coat, and the full-coated, which is the longer coat. All of the coat types should never be too long where the dog's outline is obscured or too short where you can easily see the skin of the dog.

They should have a ruff of longer hair around their neck and they should have an apron of longer hair on their chest. The coat should cover the tail well and there should be longer hair on the underside of the tail. Feathering of the hair is not always seen, but it is common in dogs with longer coats. When feathering is present, it should be present on the rear of the buttocks, hindquarters, front legs, ears and under the belly and tail.

c) Size

The Alaskan Klee Kai is a small breed of dog, and it is important to note that the breed comes in three different sizes. These sizes are:

Height:

- *Toy:* Under 13 inches (33cm)
- *Miniature:* 13 to 15 inches (33 to 38cm)
- *Standard:* 15 to 17.5 inches (38 to 44.6cm)

Weight:

- *Toy:* Under 10 pounds (4.5kg)
- *Miniature:* 10 to 15 pounds (4.5 to 6.8kg)
- *Standard:* 15 to 23 pounds (6.8 to 10.4kg)

d) Life Span

The Alaskan Klee Kai is a hardy breed that has a long lifespan. If you are planning on owning one, be prepared to dedicate between 12 to 14 years to your Klee Kai.

5. General Facts about Alaskan Klee Kai

While the breed standard helps you identify what the dog should look like, it does not really tell you a lot about the general facts surrounding them. Before you purchase your Alaskan Klee Kai, it is important to get a range of general facts about the breed.

Do Alaskan Klee Kai shed?

Yes, Alaskan Klee Kai do shed but they are considered to be average shedders during most of the year. Twice a year, they will shed their undercoat, which is called blowing coat. During this time, they become heavy shedders.

It is important to note that your climate will greatly affect how much your dog sheds. Warmer climates mean more shedding.

Are they difficult to train?

When it comes to intelligence, the Alaskan Klee Kai is in the top of their class. They are usually very clever and can learn a command easily and quickly. However, that being said, all dogs can be difficult to train if they do not have a firm owner. These are dogs that will think for themselves so you need to be on your toes with setting firm rules and being consistent with training.

Chapter Two: Understanding Alaskan Klee Kai

Are they good with children?

Alaskan Klee Kai do very well with children and tend to match their personality to the children in the house. Active children will mean an active Alaskan Klee Kai while calm, quiet children will produce a calm, quiet dog.

I do not recommend them in homes for younger children because they will not put up with any poking or prodding. They have been known to bite when mistreated, even unintentionally.

Are they good with other dogs?

Yes, Alaskan Klee Kai do very well with other dogs, especially if they are raised with them. They are generally pack oriented so they are happy being with other canines.

Are they good with non-canine pets?

While they can be trained to be tolerant of cats and other small, non-canine pets, Alaskan Klee Kai do have a strong prey drive and may chase smaller animals.

Do they make good watchdogs?

Although their size does not make them ideal as a guard dog, the Alaskan Klee Kai is an alert breed that will watch their home. For this reason, they make excellent watchdogs because they will bark alerts when they see something suspicious.

Do they do well in all climates?

Alaskan Klee Kai have a long coat but they can do well in all climates. It is important to mention that warmer climates will produce more shedding. Make sure that regardless of your climate your dog has proper shelter from the weather when it is outside including shade and a breeze in the summer.

How much do they cost?

To purchase an Alaskan Klee Kai, you should expect to pay between 1950 to 2450 USD (1540 to 1925€ or £1200 to £1500).

In addition to the price, you should expect a long wait for a puppy. Alaskan Klee Kai are quite rare, so many breeders have waiting lists of several years.

Do Alaskan Klee Kai do well in apartments?

Yes, because of their size and overall temperament, the Alaskan Klee Kai do very well in apartments. One consideration to make with an Alaskan Klee Kai is that it is a vocal dog that likes to talk. In general they do not really bark, except when on alert but they do howl, yodel and sing, which can cause problems if you have noise restrictions in your building.

Chapter 3: The Personality of the Alaskan Klee Kai

Chapter Three: The Personality of the Alaskan Klee Kai

The Alaskan Klee Kai is full of personality. With this in mind, I do stress that every dog is different. Personality will range from playful to reserved, and how a dog reacts, temperament-wise, has as much to do with how the dog is trained as genetics. When we discuss personality, we often look at the general traits that we see in the breed. However, your Alaskan Klee Kai may not have all of the same personality traits.

With that said, the Alaskan Klee Kai is known for being an intelligent breed with a stable temperament. They are usually very curious dogs and that curiosity can get them into plenty of trouble so owners need to be on their toes.

The breed is in general very loyal to their owners, but, tends to be reserved with strangers. The dogs can seem timid in strange situations and it takes a while for them to warm up to new people.

When they bond with owners Alaskan Klee Kai are very outgoing. They are affectionate and love spending time with their family.

The type of family does matter. While they can do very well with children, they need to be properly socialized to them. Always remind children how to properly handle a dog.

With other animals in the family, Alaskan Klee Kai usually gets along amazingly with other canine companions. They can be a social dog and they do enjoy being in a pack.

Non-canine pets can prove to be a challenge for the breed. If they are introduced at a young age, the breed can get along okay with smaller non-canine pets such as cats. If they do not, you may have difficulties when bringing the new pet into the home because they have a high prey drive.

Chapter Three: The Personality of the Alaskan Klee Kai

If they are not properly trained, they may attack smaller, non-canine pets

And that brings us to the territorial temperament of the breed. They will fiercely protect their homes and yards so it is important to properly socialize them. They should be accepting of people and other animals to help prevent territorial aggression in the dog. Socialization is the key to preventing this and if there are three words I stress, it is to socialize, socialize and socialize. I expand more on this topic later on in the book.

When properly socialized, an Alaskan Klee Kai is a charming little dog. They have a very even temperament and their intelligence makes them a good candidate for therapy work.

In addition to being intelligent, the Alaskan Klee Kai is a vocal little dog. They are not "yappy" like other small breeds but they love to talk. They will yip, howl, yodel and sing. They will also talk back to their owners.

Despite being such a talkative breed, the actual bark of the Alaskan Klee Kai has a "big dog" depth to it. In addition,

Chapter Three: The Personality of the Alaskan Klee Kai

this bark is usually only reserved for when they notice something suspicious.

When it comes to differences between the sexes, most owners find that there is a distinct difference in temperament. Males are generally more playful and they have a spunky personality.

Generally, males will rule the roost and will often try to be the more dominant creature in the home. They will mark their territory and they are usually more territorial than females. On the other hand, males are usually more inclined to accept new people and tend to be quite outgoing. Finally, males are often the more affectionate of the two.

Females, on the other hand, are usually more submissive than males. They are affectionate but it is not always a playful affection. They tend to be more reserved than playful.

However, bear in mind that this is not a set rule. You can have a playful and outgoing female and a submissive and reserved male. A lot of the temperament can be in the training.

In the end, you must start early with the proper knowledge to train the dog to respect you and obey you. This is covered in Chapter Seven, in the section on Training.

Chapter Four: Finding a Klee Kai

Chapter 4: Finding a Klee Kai

Chapter Four: Finding a Klee Kai

Now that you know something about the Alaskan Klee Kai, you are ready to get started on with finding a breeder and choosing your puppy. I want to note that many of the tips for finding an Alaskan Klee Kai is the same as finding any other breed of dog.

I also want to stress that when you are looking for a puppy, if you ever feel uncomfortable with the breeder, choose a different one. Trust your gut instinct and do not settle. Remember that this is an animal that you will be spending 12 to 15 years with so starting with the right breeder will ensure you have the right dog.

1. Finding a Breeder

Finding an Alaskan Klee Kai breeder can be difficult because the Alaskan Klee Kai is a rare breed. While it is starting to gain some popularity, breeders are still few and far between. What this means is that you may have to travel several days or have a puppy shipped to you.

In addition, it also means that you could be looking at a waiting list before you have a puppy. This can be frustrating when you are excited about a puppy but, the wait is worth it.

While I am not aware of every Alaskan Klee Kai breeder out there, I have compiled a list at the back of the book with breeders. This is a good place to start but I also recommend contacting the breed club, which is also listed in the resources page.

It is important to note that you should do your research on all of the breeders listed. The priorities of breeders can change and where one was excellent at one time, they may not be currently.

Chapter Four: Finding a Klee Kai

When you are looking for a breeder, it is important to look for the following traits:

1. A breeder who will answer questions.

One of the first things to look for in breeders is one that will answer your questions. Yes, breeders can be very busy. Not only do most of them have full-time jobs and family commitments but they may also have puppies to care for.

That being said, the breeder should and will usually be open to discussing the breed and potentially owning a puppy. If it is all about putting in a deposit to hold a future puppy and nothing else, then you should choose a different breeder.

2. A breeder who is active with the breed club and kennel club.

Does the breeder register her puppies with the UKC, which is the registry that accepts the Alaskan Klee Kai? Is she a member of the Alaskan Klee Kai breed club? If the breeder answers yes to both, then you can start to feel confident with them.

3. A breeder who does things with her dogs.

Make sure your Alaskan Klee Kai breeder does something with her dogs. They do not have to show, although that would be good, but they do need to do more than simply place the dogs in a kennel.

4. A breeder who can give you backgrounds on her dogs

Choose a breeder who knows the background of their dogs such as pedigree, health of the lines and where the dogs

Chapter Four: Finding a Klee Kai

came from. The breeder should also know the history of the breed and the breed standard.

If the breeder does not know much about the breed, then it is an indication that you should look elsewhere.

5. A breeder who has a puppy plan and health clearances.

Finally, look for a breeder who has a breeding plan for her overall kennel. Is she trying to breed a certain trait or just breeding for puppies? Does she have a puppy plan on how they are raised? Does she have health clearances on her dogs?

If the answer is no to one or more of those questions, choose a different breeder. Every litter should have a goal in mind that will further the breed. In addition, she should have a plan as to how the puppies will be socialized and reared.

Finally, the breeder should have dogs with their health clearances. These include:

- Eyes Certified
- Factor VII Status
- OFA Thyroid
- OFA Cardiac
- OFA Knees

Chapter Four: Finding a Klee Kai

Hold every breeder you contact to those standards and this will help narrow down a breeder for you. In addition to finding these traits in a breeder, you should also look for the following.

1. The facilities are clean.

Go to the kennel if you are able to and make sure that it is clean. If you have a breeder who will not let you see the dogs or go to the kennel, choose a different breeder. The only exception to this rule is when the breeder has young puppies in the kennel, under four to five weeks of age.

However, if there are no litters, you should be able to go and see the Alaskan Klee Kai. When you get there, check to make sure the home, kennel and grounds are clean. If you notice a lot of dirt, or the dogs are kept in poor conditions, choose a different breeder.

Puppies that come from a dirty, poorly managed kennel can have many health and behavioral problems.

2. The dogs are healthy.

Chapter Four: Finding a Klee Kai

Later on in this chapter, I discuss puppy health but it is important to use the same checklist on the adult dogs in the kennel. Remember that nursing mothers will look a little rough, especially if they are nursing a large litter. Often nursing mothers will lose weight and hair and this is completely normal.

However, the rest of the dogs should look healthy and they should have good energy. It is important not to look at just the parents of the puppies but all the dogs. If any dog looks unwell, question the breeder for it.

3. There is paperwork.

Another important thing to look for is whether there is paperwork. The breeder should have a purchase contract for new puppy owners. In addition, they should have pedigree information, certification and the health clearances for their dogs. If they do not, choose a different breeder.

4. The puppies are raised indoors.

While the Alaskan Klee Kai does enjoy time outside, it is important for socialization and health for all puppies to be raised in the home. In addition, it should not be in a backroom where the puppies can be forgotten. Puppies raised underfoot will be the most socialized puppies and this will only be a benefit to you as the pet owner.

5. They have good referrals.

Finally, make sure that the breeder has excellent referrals. While you can get the referrals from them, search around online or at dog shows to find out if anything, good or bad, has been said about your potential breeder.

Chapter Four: Finding a Klee Kai

Remember, when you are choosing your Alaskan Klee Kai breeder that if you get any negative feelings from the breeder, you should find a different one.

2. Adopting an Older Alaskan Klee Kai

Although much of this chapter is focused on finding an Alaskan Klee Kai puppy, it is important to touch on choosing an adult Alaskan Klee Kai. While it is not common, it is possible to find an older Alaskan Klee Kai. This can be a retired dog from a breeding kennel, a rescued dog, or an older puppy that the breeder has decided to let go.

Most people shy away from adopting an older Alaskan Klee Kai, but I recommend it. Adopting an older dog means that you do not have to deal with the many challenges that accompany the adoption of a puppy.

In addition, there are many pros to adopting an older Alaskan Klee Kai and these are:

- *Housebroken:* A large portion of adult dogs are housebroken when you adopt them so you do not have to housetrain the dog.

- *Less Destructive:* This varies from dog to dog but many adult Alaskan Klee Kai are trained before they go to your home. This means they are less likely to give in to bad habits such as chewing.

- *Affectionate:* Although all Alaskan Klee Kai are affectionate, many older dogs have an almost grateful demeanor with their new owners.

- *Trainable:* The old saying, "You can't teach an old dog new tricks," is wrong and you can easily teach

Chapter Four: Finding a Klee Kai

commands to old dogs. So though many adult Alaskan Klee Kai will be trained to some degree, they can always be taught new commands.

It is important to note that it does take time for an older dog to adjust to their new home and they may be withdrawn during that time. In general, it is recommended that you give the dog about one year to adjust to the change.

If you have decided on an Alaskan Klee Kai rescue, contact breeders about older dogs, or the Alaskan Klee Kai rescue at www.akkrescue.com.

3. Choosing your Alaskan Klee Kai

Once you have selected the breeder and the litter is born, it is time to select the puppy. One thing that I recommend is getting the breeder to help with the selection. Remember, she has been with the puppies since they were born so she will know which ones are more submissive and which ones are more dominant.

Often, breeders will pick for you or will give you the choice of two or three puppies. Be open about gender and color since the perfect puppy is often the one you least expect.

If you are looking for a show puppy, choose one that has the looks and temperament of the breed standard. If you are looking for a pet, you do not have to be so worried about the breed standard.

After the selections have been narrowed down between pet and show quality puppies, you can begin your choice. When choosing your puppy, take the time to watch the

Chapter Four: Finding a Klee Kai

puppies while they are playing together. Don't go in with the puppies, simply watch them.

Look for a puppy with an even temperament. Don't believe the myth that the puppy will choose you. Often, the puppy that greets people is the most dominant in the litter. While that is not always a bad thing, if you are looking for a quieter puppy, you won't get that with the dominant puppy.

Instead, look for a puppy that looks around, assesses the situation and then comes to you. This is usually the sign of a middle of the road temperament. Not too submissive where the puppy will be fearful and not too dominant where they are too pushy.

In addition to looking at temperament, look at the health of your puppy. You want to choose a puppy with the following traits:

- *Alert and energetic:* Avoid a puppy that seems lethargic. If you arrive during puppy nap time, wait until the Alaskan Klee Kai puppies are awake.

- *Bright Eyes:* Eyes should be clear of any debris and should not have any discharge. The Alaskan Klee Kai should have bright, shiny eyes.

- *Excellent Body Condition:* Look at the overall condition of the body and coat. Coat should be soft without crusty areas, dandruff or dullness. The overall body of the puppy should be fat enough such that you cannot see the ribs but skinny enough that you can feel them when you touch his sides.

- *Nose:* Nose should be shiny and wet. In addition, the puppy should have no problems breathing.

Chapter Four: Finding a Klee Kai

- ***Excellent Sight and Hearing:*** Clap your hands, encourage the puppy to chase toys and watch his reaction. If you see any signs that he cannot hear or see, you may want to choose a different puppy.

Although you will be focused on your main choice of puppy, it is important to watch all of the puppies. If you notice signs of disease in the puppies, choose a different breeder or litter.

Another trait that you should look for is a puppy that does not mind being touched and handled. If the puppy struggles or becomes fearful, you may want to discuss a different pick with your breeder.

Taking your time with the puppies, and visiting them more than once if you can, will help in choosing the right puppy for you. Remember to use the input of the breeder and be sure to follow your instincts as well.

In the end, this will be a relationship that lasts a lifetime so make sure it is the right one for you and your puppy right from the start.

Chapter 5: Getting Ready for Puppy

Chapter Five: Getting Ready for Puppy

Getting a puppy is always really exciting and part of that excitement the purchase of all the necessities. While every dog owner is different, there are some common supplies that you should purchase for your Alaskan Klee Kai.

It is important to note that the list of supplies is pretty basic and you do not need to purchase everything that is recommended by your pet store. In this chapter, I will go over the supplies that are a must have, supplies that are optional and ways for you to puppy proof your home.

1. General Supplies

A puppy does not require a lot, but it is important to have all of these items on hand before you bring it home. Never go supply shopping with your puppy. Firstly, it is very stressful for your puppy and secondly, it can open your puppy up for infections.

Essential puppy supplies are:

Feeding Bowls

Make sure that you have a water and food bowl that your puppy can easily reach. I recommend a stainless steel bowl since it can be cleaned very easily. In addition, stainless steel is less likely to have bacteria growing in it.

Collar

Purchase a flat collar for your Alaskan Klee Kai that will fit him when he comes home. Do not purchase a prong or pinch collar or a choke chain. These are not necessary for training a puppy and should never be used before a puppy is 6 months of age.

Chapter Five: Getting Ready for Puppy

Leash

There are many different leashes out there but I recommend a six-foot flat leash. Remember to use a leash that is comfortable in your hand as well as sturdy. Although you won't need it right away, you may want to purchase a 20-foot lead for later training.

Avoid retractable leads. They pose many safety problems since the dog can wander too far and get hit by a car or be attacked by another dog. In addition, the leashes themselves have caused serious injuries to owners and dogs alike.

Dog Grooming Items

While you do not need every type of dog grooming item out there, it is important to have the minimum items for grooming. These include:

- Undercoat Brush

Chapter Five: Getting Ready for Puppy

- Brush for Long Hair
- Nail Clippers
- Styptic Powder
- Toothbrush and Toothpaste
- Dog Shampoo

Crate

I strongly recommend purchasing a crate for your Alaskan Klee Kai. While some people disagree with crates, it is important to have one for housetraining. In addition, it will keep your puppy safe when you cannot watch him or are out.

One thing that many people do wrong when purchasing a crate is buy the crate according to the size of the puppy. Remember, puppies grow and purchasing a crate that fits

Chapter Five: Getting Ready for Puppy

only your puppy will end up costing you a lot more money as you have to upgrade the crate as your puppy grows.

The general rule of thumb is to purchase a crate where your full grown dog can stand up in and turn around without problem. It should also have enough room for him to lie down comfortably.

When purchasing your first crate, purchase with the adult dog in mind. Also, buy one with crate dividers. You can use the dividers to make the crate smaller for your puppy and then remove the dividers as he grows.

One word of caution with crates is to never crate a dog with his collar on. It is quite easy for the dog's collar to catch on the crate bars and choke the dog.

Toys

While many people think of toys as being optional, I always recommend that you have some on hand. When your puppy begins chewing on something, you can reach for a toy and distract your Alaskan Klee Kai from chewing.

Make sure you choose toys that are recommended for your dog's breed and size. Also, choose puppy toys for puppies as their teeth can chew through a lot of items and this can cause choking hazards.

Chapter Five: Getting Ready for Puppy

Cleaning Supplies:

While not really a puppy item, cleaning supplies are necessary when bringing a puppy home. Purchase carpet and floor cleaners that contain enzymes to remove odors that would attract further soiling.

Also, stock up on paper towels as you will need them.

Dog Bed

Finally, purchase a dog bed or a crate bed for your puppy. Even if you allow your puppy up on the furniture, it is good to have something for him to lie on in the crate.

As you can see, you really do not need a lot and purchasing them before bringing puppy home will help keep your expenses to a minimum.

2. Additional Supplies

There are a few additional supplies that are optional. Consider them only if you feel it is necessary to your situation.

Puppy Training Pads

These are pads that you put out for puppy to go to the bathroom on. I personally do not use puppy training pads as it makes housetraining harder since you have to teach the dog to go on the pads, and then go outside.

However, if you do not have immediate access to the outdoors, such as living in a sky scraper, or if you have limited ability to get a puppy out, puppy pads can be the answer.

Chapter Five: Getting Ready for Puppy

Baby Gates

These are necessary if you want to close off rooms of your house when puppy comes home. I recommend them so you can open up rooms only when you can trust a puppy completely. They are not, however, 100% necessary.

Stress Reducing Items

There has been a huge push for stress-reducing blankets, toys and sprays for puppies, however, I find that they are a waste of money. Instead of purchasing these, simply take a small doggie blanket to the breeder's home and have her rub it on mom and siblings. That will provide your puppy with a lot of comfort for a fraction of the cost.

Vitamins

While there are a lot of benefits when you give your dog vitamins, you should never do it without the direction of your vet. Some vitamins are toxic when given in high

Chapter Five: Getting Ready for Puppy

doses so you want to avoid inadvertently poisoning your Alaskan Klee Kai.

When you are choosing your puppy supplies, take your time and start with the essentials, including food and treats. After that, anything else is just an added way to spoil your puppy.

3. Puppy Proofing your Home

The final thing to touch upon in regards to getting ready for your puppy is puppy proofing your house. Puppies are naturally curious and the Alaskan Klee Kai is more so. This is a breed that is known for its curiosity and that curiosity can be harmful.

To prevent that from happening, it is important to puppy proof your home before your Alaskan Klee Kai comes home. To properly puppy proof your home, follow the tips below:

Chapter Five: Getting Ready for Puppy

1. Put away any hazardous items

Pick up and lock away any items that can be hazardous to your Alaskan Klee Kai. This includes:

- Household cleaners
- Vitamins
- Medication
- Vehicle fluids, such as antifreeze
- Salts for ice or water softening
- Pool chemicals
- Tobacco products

2. Crawl around

Take the time to crawl around your home before your puppy arrives and then once or twice a week. Look at things from puppy's vantage point. Pick up small clips, tags, paper, and anything else that can be a choking hazard for the puppy.

Also, keep clothes picked up. It can be surprising but some articles of clothing, such as socks, can pose a choking hazard for a puppy.

3. Put knick knacks up high

While you may love having your ornaments on tables and shelves, look at what your Alaskan Klee Kai can reach. If he can get at it, move it up out of reach. This will prevent the item from being broken and your puppy from getting

Chapter Five: Getting Ready for Puppy

hurt. It does not have to be permanent but only until your puppy learns what he is and is not allowed to touch.

4. Close off access to standing water

Close toilet seat lids, drain tubs and sinks, and block off any access to a pool if you have one. Standing water can be very tempting for an Alaskan Klee Kai, however, young puppies cannot swim well if at all, they could drown.

5. Tie up those electrical cords and drape cords

Electrical cords are always very tempting for a puppy and are often chewed. Always tape your cords out of reach of your puppy. Also, look for cords that dangle from furniture as the puppy may knock a lamp down on himself when playing with a cord.

In addition to electrical cords, pull up the drape or blind cords. These can lead to strangulation if the puppy gets caught in them.

6. Keep garbage out of reach or in a puppy proof container

Another tempting item for puppies is the garbage can. Always keep it put up where the puppy cannot get at it and make sure you empty it every night, especially if you are letting puppy sleep outside of his crate.

7. Block off stairs

Even if you allow your Alaskan Klee Kai upstairs with you, block off the stairs at both the top and the bottom. Puppies are uncoordinated and can find the stairs difficult to maneuver. It is quite common for a puppy to fall down

Chapter Five: Getting Ready for Puppy

stairs. To prevent this, keep the stairs blocked and off limits.

8. Keep doors closed

Any door or window leading outside should be kept closed if the puppy can access it. Remember that Alaskan Klee Kai do have a high prey drive so they will chase after small animals. Even if there is nothing outside to catch their interest, an open door presents an opportunity to explore.

9. Check the outdoors

In addition to puppy proofing your house, make sure that you check the outdoors. Look for openings in the fence, items that can be hazardous to your Alaskan Klee Kai puppy, such as drainpipes, pools or other items in your yard that can present a risk.

If there are, pick up all the hazardous items and fence or block off the rest such as the pool or drain pipes. The goal is to make the outdoors as safe as the indoors.

10. Look at your plants

Finally, look at the plants that you have in your home and garden. Many plants are poisonous to dogs so avoid having

Chapter Five: Getting Ready for Puppy

them in your home. If you do have them, make sure they are out of your puppy's reach.

In the end, puppy proofing is simply keeping your house neat and tidy. Everyone in the home should work with you to keep the space clean and you should constantly reassess if your house is still safe for your puppy.

Staying on top of puppy proofing will make sure that your puppy is always safe.

4. Toxic Plants

Since I am discussing puppy proofing your home, here is a list of plants that you should avoid having both inside and out in the garden. All of the plants in this list are poisonous in varying degrees, including deadly, to your Alaskan Klee Kai.

Aconite	Emerald Feather	Nightshade
Aloe Vera	English Ivy	Oaks
Amaryllis	Eucalyptus	Oleander
Apple Leaf Croton	European Bittersweet	Onions
Arrow grasses	False Fax	Oriental Lily
Asparagus Fern	False Hellebore	Peace Lily
Atropa belladonna	Fan Weed	Peach Tree
Autumn Crocus	Fiddle-leaf Fig	Pencil Cactus
Azalea	Field Peppergrass	Philodendrons
Baby's Breath	Florida Beauty	Plumosa Fern
Baneberry	Foxglove	Pokeweed
Bird of Paradise	Fruit Salad Plant	Poinsettia
Black Locust	Geranium	Poison Hemlock
Bloodroot	German Ivy	Poison Ivy
Box	Giant Dumb Cane	Poison Oak
Branching Ivy	Glacier Ivy	Potato Plant
Buckeye	Gold Dust	Pothos

Chapter Five: Getting Ready for Puppy

	Dracaena	
Buddhist Pine	Golden Pothos	Precatory Bean
Buttercup	Hahn's Self-Branching Ivy	Primrose
Caladium	Heartland Philodendron	Rattle box
Calla Lily	Holly	Red Emerald
Carolina Jessamine	Horse Chestnut	Red Princess
Castor Bean	Horse Nettle	Red-Margined Dracaena
Ceriman	Hurricane Plant	Rhododendron
Charming Dieffenbachia	Indian Rubber Plant	Rhubarb
Cherry Tree	Iris	Ribbon Plant
Chinaberry Tree	Jack-in-the-Pulpit	Rosary Pea
Chinese Evergreen	Japanese Show Lily	Saddle Leaf Philodendron
Chock Cherries	Jatropha	Sago Palm
Christmas Berry	Jerusalem Cherry	Satin Pothos
Christmas Rose	Jimsonweed	Schefflera
Cineraria	Kalan Choe	Skunk Cabbage
Clematis	Labarum	Silver Pothos
Common Privet	Lacey Tree Philodendron	Smartweeds
Cordatum	Lantana	Snow-on-the-Mountain
Corn Cockle	Laurels	Sorghum
Corn Plant	Lily of the Valley	Spotted Dumb Cane
Cornstalk Plant	Lupines	Star of Bethlehem
Cowbane	Madagascar Dragon Tree	String of Pearls
Cow Cockle	Manchineel Tree	Striped Dracaena
Cowslip	Marble Queen	Sweetheart Ivy
Croton	Marijuana	Swiss Cheese Plant

Chapter Five: Getting Ready for Puppy

Cuban Laurel	Matrimony Vine	Taro Vine
Cutleaf Philodendron	May Apple	Tiger Lily
Cycads	Mexican Breadfruit	Tomato Plant
Cyclamen	Milk Vetch	Tree Philodendron
Daffodil	Miniature Croton	Tropic Snow Dieffenbachia
Daphne	Mistletoe	Velvet Grass
Death Camas	Monk's Hood	Weeping Fig
Delphinium	Moonseed	Wild Black Cherry
Devil's Ivy	Morning Glory	Wild Radish
Dieffenbachia,	Mother-in Law's Tongue	Wisteria
Dracaena Palm	Mountain Mahogany	Wood Aster
Dragon Tree	Mustards	Yellow Jessamine
Dumb Cane	Narcissus	Yellow Oleander
Dutchman's Breeches	Needlepoint Ivy	Yellow Pine Flax
Elephant Ears	Nephthytis	Yew

Chapter 6: Bringing Puppy Home

Chapter Six: Bringing Puppy Home

So you have selected your puppy, purchased the supplies and waited the long weeks before your puppy comes home. It can be an exciting time but it is important to remember that picking him up properly is just as important as caring for your Alaskan Klee Kai.

The pickup can greatly affect the puppy's development and your bond.

In this chapter, I will go over everything you need to know about bringing your Alaskan Klee Kai puppy home.

1. The Day of Pick Up

The day that you pick up your Alaskan Klee Kai is a very exciting day. If you have not been lucky to find a breeder with puppies, it often means that you have waited months and even years to get your puppy. It can be difficult to keep the excitement down but it is important to do so for the puppy, who will be scared during this time.

When you are picking up your Alaskan Klee Kai, it is important to start taking steps to pick up your puppy before you even go. If it is possible, send a blanket to the breeder a few days before and ask her to rub it on his siblings and mom. If it isn't possible, bring the blanket with you when you pick him up.

Although picking up a puppy is a wonderful experience, I recommend that you leave children at home. This can be a very stressful time for your Alaskan Klee Kai and the excitement of children can overwhelm the puppy. Before you leave, have everything set up so you can simply bring him home and take him to his safe place.

In addition, place a crate in your car for your Alaskan Klee Kai to travel home in. If you have someone else coming

Chapter Six: Bringing Puppy Home

with you to pick up the puppy, they can carry him in their lap, but he should never be loose in the car or held by the driver.

Once you arrive at the breeder's house, spend time with the sibling, mom and the breeder. I recommend having any last minute questions written down so you won't forget to ask. It is important to build a relationship with your breeder as they can be a valuable resource for you.

After you leave the breeder, go straight home. Do not stop to visit a friend or go to a pet store. Every place you stop opens your Alaskan Klee Kai up for exposure to disease and extra stress. Keep the trip calm and do not worry, your puppy will soon be able to go to friends' houses.

In the car, keep an eye on your Alaskan Klee Kai. Many puppies experience motion sickness in cars. If you see your puppy's nose drooping towards the floor as well as drooling and wrinkled lips, pull over and allow him time to get over his car sickness. He may throw up but that is perfectly normal.

Chapter Six: Bringing Puppy Home

If you do have to stop, whether for a potty break or because he is car sick, try to stop at secluded spots where you won't expect a lot of dogs. Take him to an area to potty and then immediately pick him up. Avoid other dogs as you do not know which ones have been properly vaccinated.

When you get home, immediately take him outside to the bathroom. Often puppies will sniff around the yard and then go to the bathroom. Once he has gone to the bathroom, take him to a quiet room.

Sit with him and allow him the opportunity to explore his surroundings. Alaskan Klee Kai puppies differ when they are in their new homes. Some will want to play and run around, others want to sleep. Follow the cues of your puppy so you do not frighten him.

Introduce him slowly to family members and keep all interactions with the new puppy calm. During the first few days, you will find your Alaskan Klee Kai sleeps a lot, but this will change as he becomes familiar with his home.

Although it may seem cruel, start the exact way that you will be behaving when he is an adult. Keep to a schedule for housetraining and stick to rules. If your Alaskan Klee Kai will not be allowed on the furniture, do not let him up as a puppy.

Keep the puppy confined to one area and then slowly open up your home to your puppy as he becomes more confident. The key to introducing your puppy to his new home is in being calm, progressing slowly and creating those rules and schedules.

Chapter Six: Bringing Puppy Home

2. Introducing your Alaskan Klee Kai to other Family Members

Once you get your puppy home, it is time to introduce him to the other residents in your home. While the first instinct is to rush in and introduce him to everyone, your Alaskan Klee Kai can become very frightened. In addition, the puppy can become overwhelmed and begin to shut down.

Since you want all introductions to be positive, I recommend making the introductions as calm as possible. In addition, let the puppy have time to acclimatize to his new home.

One of the best things that you can do for your puppy when you bring him home is to allow him to rest in a quiet room. After he has had some time to adjust, start bringing in people to meet him.

Other animals in the home can wait a day or two. There is no rush and you want to do the introductions properly to prevent any lasting problems in your Alaskan Klee Kai.

a) Children

If you have brought your children to pick up your puppy, the introduction will be done at the breeders and nothing will change. On the other hand if your children were at home when you picked up your Alaskan Klee Kai, then introductions have to be made at home.

My rule of thumb is to bring your Alaskan Klee Kai puppy home, let him go outside and then place him in a separate room where he can relax. Give him a chance to adjust to the new smells before you bring your children in to greet him.

Chapter Six: Bringing Puppy Home

For younger children, introduce them one at a time to help minimize the amount of stimulation the puppy has. If you have older children, you can introduce them all at once.

When you are introducing your Alaskan Klee Kai puppy to children, have your child come into the room and sit down on the floor. Do not rush the puppy and do not place the puppy in your child's lap.

Instead, give the child treats to feed the puppy and allow the puppy to approach on his own terms. Tell the child to stay calm and quiet so the puppy will not get frightened.

Alaskan Klee Kai naturally love children so the puppy should naturally gravitate to the child. When the puppy does greet the child, let the child pet the Alaskan Klee Kai calmly.

Keep meetings short and build on them. In addition, over the first few days, make all interactions with the children calm and quiet. As the puppy gets used to the sounds of children, you can start introducing play times.

Make clear what the rules are about the puppy so that the children know exactly how to treat him. Make sure your children understand the following rules:

- Be calm around the puppy.
- Do not hold onto him when he wants to go.
- Never hit or pinch the puppy.
- Don't pull on the ears or tail.
- Gently pet the puppy.
- Use toys to play with the puppy.

Chapter Six: Bringing Puppy Home

As you train your Alaskan Klee Kai puppy, make sure that you include your child in the training and socializing. By doing this, it will teach your Alaskan Klee Kai that he has to listen and be respectful to the children as well as to you.

b) Other Pets

Introducing your Alaskan Klee Kai puppy to other pets in the home is something that should be done gradually. Remember that the animals in the home were there first and they can have some behavioral problems with a new puppy.

To prevent these problems, make sure that you make the meetings short and you do not force any relationships. The animals in your home will sort out their hierarchy on their own.

When introducing other pets, it is important to follow these rules:

Chapter Six: Bringing Puppy Home

1. Keep the puppy confined

The first rule is that you should always keep your puppy confined when you bring him home. Place your Alaskan Klee Kai into a quiet room. This will keep your puppy safe while making your resident pet feel confident.

When you are bringing the puppy out of his room, confine the resident dog unless you are taking the time to introduce them. However, I only recommend the latter after your older pet has had time to adjust to the new puppy.

2. Allow door sniffing

Or crate sniffing. What this means is that you should allow your resident pet to sniff at the crate or the door where the puppy is. Don't let them be pushy and if your puppy starts to look stressed, stop the behavior.

Sniffing at the door will help your pet become acquainted with the puppy while there is a safe obstacle between the pet and the puppy.

3. Set up the meeting

Whenever you are going to do a meeting, it is important to set it up first. Never bring in a puppy and then allow your resident pet to make the introduction. Instead, wait until your pet is calm before you make the introductions. This will help promote a positive experience for both your new Alaskan Klee Kai and your resident pet.

4. Make the resident pet equate the puppy with positives

When you are doing the introductions, always make your resident pet feel the most affection. Give him lots of praise for greeting nicely and make sure that you give your

Chapter Six: Bringing Puppy Home

resident pet plenty of treats. The more you praise your resident pet, the more he will think the new Alaskan Klee Kai puppy is a positive thing.

5. Let cats greet on their own terms

While you can control the meetings between a dog and puppy, it can be difficult to control the meeting between a puppy and cat. Often, puppies find cats interesting and will try to chase the cat or play with him. When this happens, the cat will usually react.

The best thing to do is allow the cat to watch the Alaskan Klee Kai puppy from his own vantage points. Praise, treat and pet the cat when you are able so he will be comfortable with the new excitement in the home.

After a few weeks, start bringing your cat down from his perches, but only when the puppy is calm. Do not introduce the cat in the middle of a play session. Always make sure that you have control of your Alaskan Klee Kai to prevent him from chasing the cat.

It may take time but eventually, your Alaskan Klee Kai will come to make friends with the cat, but it will always be on the cat's terms.

6. Make the older pet the primary pet

What this means is that your resident pet should have more rights than the puppy. They should be fed first, greet them when you get home first and you should always allow the resident pet to enter or exit first.

As the animals become more acquainted with each other, you can start offering attention and everything else equally

Chapter Six: Bringing Puppy Home

but for the first few months, make the current resident feel extra special.

7. Be patient

Finally, be patient with your pets. Remember that this is a big adjustment for them and that they may not warm up quickly. In fact, many times it can take up to 6 months for the puppy to be accepted by the resident pets. For cats, it can take up to a year.

3. Socialization and the First Few Weeks

Later in this book, I will discuss socialization for your Alaskan Klee Kai, however, some matters need to be touched upon right now. Socialization is an important aspect of your puppy's life and it actually starts from the moment he is born.

Before he comes home, your breeder should have taken the time to socialize him. In addition, the mom and siblings of

Chapter Six: Bringing Puppy Home

your Alaskan Klee Kai will also socialize him and teach him puppy manners.

However, after he comes home, it is up to you to properly socialize your Alaskan Klee Kai. One problem that I see countless owners deal with is improper socialization. Many trainers will recommend puppy classes after 12 weeks of age and won't stress socialization until after those classes start.

While puppy kindergarten is important and I strongly recommend it for the Alaskan Klee Kai, the puppy should be socialized well before 12 weeks. The crucial time period for socialization is between 3 to 12 weeks of age.

Obviously, between 3 and 8 weeks of age, your puppy will be socialized at the breeders, however, between 8 to 12 weeks, you need to take the time to socialize them at home. The reason why this is a crucial period is because during this time, puppies are less fearful and more open to new experiences.

At 12 to 13 weeks of age, some puppies sooner, others later, the Alaskan Klee Kai puppy will start to become more cautious about new things and this can make socializing harder.

The main problem with this window is the fact that your Alaskan Klee Kai cannot go to many places until he has had his second set of vaccinations. However, you can bring the socialization to him.

During the first four weeks at home, take the time to socialize your puppy to a range of different stimuli in the house. For example, vacuum, watch television, and have guests over.

Chapter Six: Bringing Puppy Home

Make sure that you touch your puppy and handle him often so he can become socialized to your touch. After your puppy is 12 weeks old, or has had his second set of shots, get out and get socializing in other locations.

For more information on socialization, read the chapter on socializing your Alaskan Klee Kai.

Chapter Seven: Caring for your Alaskan Klee Kai

Chapter 7: Caring for your Alaskan Klee Kai

Chapter Seven: Caring for your Alaskan Klee Kai

Caring for your Alaskan Klee Kai does not have to be something that is overly complicated. They are a guardian but also a companion breed and as such, they do not require a lot of daily care. Feeding, some light grooming and exercise is really all that is needed.

The rest of the time, the Alaskan Klee Kai is a wonderful breed to own and really isn't too demanding. They will happily spend their day with their owners, whether that is curled up on their lap or out walking with them.

In this chapter, I will go over everything you need to know about taking care of your dog on the day to day.

1. Daily Care

Daily care of the Alaskan Klee Kai is very simple, as I mentioned, and really is just about setting up a schedule with your Alaskan Klee Kai. Remember, when the dog is young, he won't be able to be left alone for long periods, expect about 2 hours between each potty break.

As your Alaskan Klee Kai gets older, you will be able to leave him for longer periods without having any problems with him going in the house.

With that being said, the schedule that you should follow with the Alaskan Klee Kai should have the following items on it.

Feeding

Dogs should be fed every day and how often really depends on your dog's age. However, I always recommend a minimum of two feeding times per day; usually morning and afternoon/evening.

Chapter Seven: Caring for your Alaskan Klee Kai

In addition to feeding, you should offer your dog treats daily. Give them things they enjoy as both a reward and a way to keep them from being bored.

Watering

I go over both food and water in the chapter on feeding your Alaskan Klee Kai but make sure that your dog always has access to clean water. They should be given more water in summer and I mention the amounts required in the chapter on feeding.

Grooming

As discussed later in this chapter, the Alaskan Klee Kai is a breed of dog that does require a great deal of grooming. They do not shed excessively but as with all other breeds, grooming also attends to a secondary function of removing dead skin cells (dandruff) and therefore avoids the allergies that can result from excessive dead cell build up. Dogs that live in warmer climates, or dogs that reside inside, will shed more than those that do not.

Expect to groom your dog about every other day. When your Alaskan Klee Kai is shedding, you should expect to do so daily.

Training and Socializing

In the chapter on socializing, I stress the importance of both. Remember that the Alaskan Klee Kai can be territorial if they are allowed so it is important to continue socialization throughout the life of your dog.

In addition, training can be an excellent way to bond with your Alaskan Klee Kai. It will keep him from being bored,

Chapter Seven: Caring for your Alaskan Klee Kai

and will also keep him from breaking commands, which can happen when the dogs are older.

Spend about 10 to 15 minutes a day doing active training and socialization with your puppy. You will be pleased that you did.

Exercise

In addition to training and socializing, you should take your Alaskan Klee Kai for some exercise. This can be through a walk, playing fetch or a range of other physical activities. Later in this chapter, I will go over exercising your Alaskan Klee Kai.

Bathroom Breaks

Another factor with daily care is taking your Alaskan Klee Kai outside for potty breaks. When your Alaskan Klee Kai is a puppy, you will need to let him out every few hours. The general rule with puppies is that they can hold their bladder for one hour for every month of age.

So with that in mind, you should expect to take your puppy outside every 2 hours when he is 8 weeks old. Bear in mind that some puppies can hold their bladder longer and some

Chapter Seven: Caring for your Alaskan Klee Kai

for not as long so do not use the general rule as a hard rule. Also, do not expect your puppy to be fully housetrained until they are 6 months of age.

With adult Alaskan Klee Kai, you should expect to take your dog out 4 to 5 times a day, if not more. This would be immediately when he gets up, again 20 minutes after each meal, and once before bed.

Quality Time

Finally, you should put quality time into your schedule every day. An Alaskan Klee Kai thrives when he can spend time with his owner. This does not have to be time consuming but can be as simple as sitting down and petting him while you watch TV.

Take the time to make your Alaskan Klee Kai happy and you will find he is a wonderful companion you love spending time with.

In the end, daily care can take you all of an hour a day and many of the things you need to do for your Alaskan Klee Kai can be done when you are doing other things.

2. Exercise

Exercise is an important part of caring for your Alaskan Klee Kai and will be one of the deciding factors on how happy your Klee Kai is.

First, I want to emphasize that this is not a lazy breed. While they are happy to curl up with their owners while they are watching television, the Alaskan Klee Kai has a lot of energy. They need to be exercised and without the proper amount, they can become difficult to handle.

Chapter Seven: Caring for your Alaskan Klee Kai

In general, I strongly recommend that you take your Alaskan Klee Kai for two to three walks per day. These walks should be between 20 to 30 minutes each. Despite their size, the Alaskan Klee Kai can make an excellent jogging partner but remember these recommendations for walking and jogging are for adult dogs. Puppies should never be jogging companions and they will get tired much faster so they will not need long walks.

With exercise, it is important to give your Alaskan Klee Kai some time off leash. Only do this when you have a fenced yard or secure area for your dog. While they are not known for being escape artists, they will try to run away when they see something that triggers their prey drive.

In addition, the Alaskan Klee Kai has Siberian Husky in it, which is a breed known for wandering. It is important to find an appropriate place to give the Alaskan Klee Kai enough time off the leash. Play fetch, take him to a dog park, or simply let him play in his backyard. The key is to let him have 20 to 30 minutes of off-leash play time.

Another important point is to exercise your Alaskan Klee Kai's mind. These are very intelligent dogs and they can become a handful when they do not have things to do. Give them access to toys when you are away.

Also make sure that they have puzzle toys to play with. This will keep them busy as well as keep their mind active.

3. Grooming

During warmer months, or seasons when they blow coat, (another term used to describe heavy shedding), you will need to make your grooming a daily occurrence.

Chapter Seven: Caring for your Alaskan Klee Kai

Although many people view grooming as a chore, it can actually be a very pleasant activity that you do with your Alaskan Klee Kai. It provides you with an opportunity to bond with your dog and also creates a period of quiet time for your Alaskan Klee Kai.

In addition, it helps you stay on top of health problems with your dog since part of grooming is checking over its health.

With grooming, I recommend that you groom your puppy daily. Take the time to touch his paws, tail, head and body so he gets used to being handled. Make it a positive experience with treats and praise. If you start off on the right tone with your puppy, grooming will be easy and enjoyable for both of you.

When we look at grooming, we should actually focus on several areas, which I will go into in detail.

a) Bathing

Bathing is not something that needs to be done frequently with an Alaskan Klee Kai. It is not known for being an overly smelly dog so avoid frequent bathing. The more you bathe your

Chapter Seven: Caring for your Alaskan Klee Kai

dog, the more the skin will dry out, which will damage the coat and cause you more problems.

Bathing once every two to three months is usually more than enough to keep your Alaskan Klee Kai clean. When bathing, use a dog shampoo that is made for your dog's coat color. Avoid human shampoos as the many chemicals and additives to human shampoo often dry out a dog's coat.

Bathe your Alaskan Klee Kai in warm water and make sure that you always rinse the coat completely. Leaving shampoo residue can lead to dandruff.

b) Nail Clipping

Clipping your Alaskan Klee Kai's nails is another important part of regular care, although it is not usually daily care. Nail clipping, and the frequency of clipping, differs from dog to dog. Some dogs require their nails to be clipped once a week, others once a month. Where they live, the type of flooring will affect how often they need their nails clipped.

To properly clip your Alaskan Klee Kai's nails, you can either use a traditional clipper, which has a sharp blade or a Dremel (rotary polishing) tool. I prefer a Dremel as it keeps the nail smooth. If the quick is cut, which is the vein in each nail, the Dremel tool will cauterize the cut and prevent bleeding.

When you are clipping the nails, hold the paw firmly in one hand. Holding the tool at a 90 degree angle with the nail, grind or make a small cut. Never take a lot of nail off with the first cut, instead, make small cuts and slowly work your way back.

Chapter Seven: Caring for your Alaskan Klee Kai

In dogs with clear nails, you should be able to see the quick as a pink line in the center of the nail. In dogs with black nails, simply cut back until you start to see a grey oval in the nail. This is the main indication that you are close to the quick.

If you happen to cut the quick, do not worry. You can stop the bleeding by dipping the nail in corn starch or styptic powder. Although your dog will yelp in pain, it is important to cut another nail on the dog before you end the session. The reason for this is so the dog does not end a nail clipping session on a negative. End every grooming session with a positive so your Alaskan Klee Kai realizes that grooming is a positive thing.

One point to mention with nail trimming is to also take the time to look at the hairs on your Alaskan Klee Kai's paws and carefully trim any hair that is growing between the toes. The goal is to create a clean paw.

c) Brushing

As I have mentioned, the Alaskan Klee Kai should be brushed on a daily or every other day basis. Brushing has a lot of benefits and these are:

- Allows you to bond with your dog.

- Helps distribute the oil through your dog's coat.

- Removes dead skin.

- Removes excess hair.

- Allows you an opportunity to check the health of your dog's body.

Chapter Seven: Caring for your Alaskan Klee Kai

When your Alaskan Klee Kai is young, it is important to spend time simply brushing and petting your puppy in a grooming session. This will make grooming very positive for your Alaskan Klee Kai and will ensure that he enjoys it. It will also give you the opportunity to look over your dog and make sure that he is healthy and happy.

Make sure that you choose a brush that matches your dog's coat. Also make sure that you have an undercoat brush since this is the main coat that sheds. Brush your dog going in the direction of hair growth, not against it. Use a smaller brush for the ears and head.

Brushing should only take 10 to 20 minutes. End every brushing session with a treat so your dog will look forward to being groomed.

d) Ears

Although Alaskan Klee Kai are not prone to ear infections, it is important to clean the ears of your dog on a weekly basis. In many cases, the strong dog odor comes from a dog's ears. Keeping the ears clean will minimize the odor.

To clean the ears, never use cotton swabs. Sticking a swab down the ear can lead to ear damage that can be very difficult to repair. In addition, the Q-tips will often push debris down into the ear and this will cause more problems.

Instead, soak a cotton ball in ear cleaning solution. Place the swab into the ear and then massage the ear area. Remove the swab and wipe the outside of the ear canal and the overall ear until they are clean.

Check the ears for any hair and trim or comb it if there are mats in the hair or hair grown down inside the ear canal.

Chapter Seven: Caring for your Alaskan Klee Kai

And that is all there is to cleaning your Alaskan Klee Kai's ears. Remember to never put anything down the ears that is smaller than your finger and if you see any type of unusual discharge, take your dog to the vet.

e) Teeth

The final area that should be groomed on your Alaskan Klee Kai is the teeth. Unlike people, dogs do not need their teeth brushed several times a day. Instead, you can brush them about two or three times a week.

When you brush your dog's teeth, make sure that you use a canine toothbrush. If you have not introduced your dog to brushing, start with just the toothbrush, no toothpaste.

Never use human toothpaste as it can cause stomach upset in dogs. Instead, use baking soda or a canine toothpaste.

With brushing the teeth, all you need to brush are the outside surfaces of the teeth. The top of each tooth, as well as the inside of the teeth, are kept clean by the dog's tongue.

Brushing should only take a few minutes but make sure you offer a treat after the brushing so the dog feels it is positive.

And that is all you need to know about grooming your Alaskan Klee Kai. While it may seem like a lot, it is really only a few minutes each day.

4. Training

Several times throughout this book, I go over the training difficulties of Alaskan Klee Kai. While I want to stress that you should train your Alaskan Klee Kai using alpha style

Chapter Seven: Caring for your Alaskan Klee Kai

training, the present section is not about how to train your dog.

Instead, it is about the essential commands that your Alaskan Klee Kai should know and how to teach those commands to your dog.

When I am training any dog, I use a small treat morsel that is soft and does not require a lot of chewing. Hard treats that need to be chewed break the training session too much. The dog has to focus more on chewing than on training.

The best training treat I have ever used is hotdogs but you can also use veggie dogs as a vegetarian option. Slice the hotdogs into pieces that are no larger than your pinkie nail. These have tons of flavor and are easy to chew. In addition, their smell is perfect for baiting a dog into position. The dog will always follow your hand when you are holding a hot dog treat.

When you are training your Alaskan Klee Kai, keep him on the leash the entire time. This will prevent him from wandering away when he is bored.

In addition, there are always some sequences that you should always follow. First, never give the command more than once. If you repeat the command, your Alaskan Klee Kai will decide that he does not have to listen.

Second, give praise before the treat. You want your Alaskan Klee Kai to be working for praise not food.

Chapter Seven: Caring for your Alaskan Klee Kai

Finally, always touch the dog's collar when he has completed the command.

The reason for the latter is to let the dog know that touching the collar is not bad. Often, when we give a command, such as come, sit and heel, it is because we want to gain control of them. If we do not train a dog to become familiar with having their leash touched, the dog may get into the habit of running from you when you go to grab his collar.

a) "Sit!"

"Sit" is one of the first commands your Alaskan Klee Kai will need to learn. To train "sit." do the following:

1. Have your dog stand in front of you so he is facing you.

2. Place a treat in your right hand and place it near his nose. Do not let him get at the treat.

3. Give the command, never repeat the command, just say it once, "sit."

4. Bring the treat up and over his head slowly. His muzzle should follow and his bottom should drop.

5. If he tries to step back to follow the treat, restrict his movement with the leash and repeat the action. You are either too high or going too quickly. Do not repeat the command.

6. If he still does not sit, apply a small amount of pressure to his hind quarters to make his butt drop.

Chapter Seven: Caring for your Alaskan Klee Kai

7. The second his bottom touches the ground in a sit, praise the dog, touch his collar and then give him the treat.

b) "Stay!"

"Stay" is another command that is taught when your puppy is young. It is an important command that can be used in conjunction to a number of different commands. To train stay, do the following:

1. Place your dog into a sit or down position.

2. Give the dog the command, "stay."

3. Place your hand in front of his nose, palm facing the dog.

4. Remove your hand and take a step back.

5. If he breaks the "stay." give a firm correction with your voice and place him directly back where you gave the "stay" command.

6. If he does not move, take a step back to him and praise, touch his collar and treat him.

7. Repeat the process, slowly going further away from him and making him wait for longer as the training progresses.

c) "Down"

Teaching "down" refers to teaching your Alaskan Klee Kai to lie down. This should be taught after your dog has learned the sit command since you will often put them into a "down" from a "sit." especially when they are first learning the command. To train "down." do the following:

Chapter Seven: Caring for your Alaskan Klee Kai

1. Place your dog into a "sit" in front of you so he is facing you.

2. Place a treat in your right hand and place it near his nose. Do not let him get at the treat.

3. Give the command, "down."

4. Lower the treat to the floor between his paws and move the treat away from the dog. Move slowly so the dog will follow the treat.

5. If he tries to step forward to follow the treat, you are either going too quickly or moving too far forward. Restrict his movement with the leash and repeat the action. Do not repeat the command.

6. If he still does not lie down, apply a small amount of pressure to his shoulders to encourage him to lie down.

7. When he is lying down, give the dog praise, touch his collar and give him the treat.

d) "Come"

This is one of the most important commands that you can teach your Alaskan Klee Kai, and is also one of the hardest. This is the command where you will need to have some trust in your dog. However, when you are first training the Alaskan Klee Kai, you will need to keep him on the leash.

When you are teaching "come," it is important to never use the command for punishment. What this means is that you should never tell your Alaskan Klee Kai to "come" when he has done something wrong, and then punish him when

Chapter Seven: Caring for your Alaskan Klee Kai

he does. The dog will learn that "come" is a bad thing and he won't come at any other time.

Instead, make it the most wonderful thing that your dog can do. Heap praise on him and give him lots of treats. To encourage your Alaskan Klee Kai to come, clap your hands, be exciting and interesting and your Alaskan Klee Kai will come running.

You can train "come" in two different ways, one is when you place him in a "sit" and "stay." and then call him to "come." This is a focused "come" and while it is useful, it shouldn't be the only way you teach "come." Remember that 90% of the time, your dog will need to come when there is something more interesting to look at.

The other way to train "come" is when he is distracted. This can be taught on a leash as well. To do any type of leash training to "come." you should do the following:

1. Place your dog on the leash. Either have him do a "sit"–"stay" or let him forage out ahead of you. I recommend using a 20-foot lead for this so you can introduce come at different distances.

2. If he is in a "sit" –"stay." walk away from the dog and then give the command for "come." If he is forging ahead, wait until your Alaskan Klee Kai is distracted.

3. Give the command, "come," and then encourage the dog to come to you by clapping your thighs, being excited and so on. Wave a treat out for him. Do not repeat the command.

4. If the dog does not come, start winding him in with the leash.

Chapter Seven: Caring for your Alaskan Klee Kai

5. When the dog reaches you, either on his own or by being reeled in, use the treat to guide him into a "sit" without giving the command.

6. Praise the dog, touch his collar and treat.

7. Continue training "come" over several weeks. After your puppy becomes adept at "come" at a few feet, increase the distance slightly. The goal is to work up until your dog can be 100 or more feet from you and still "come" when called, whether on the leash or off.

e) "Focus"

Not everyone teaches "focus" but I strongly recommend it because it is just a quick reminder to the dog that they need to focus on me. To teach "focus." all you need is a treat.

1. Have the dog sit or stand in front of you.

2. Place a treat in your hand and place it against his nose. Do not let him take it.

3. Raise the treat slowly to your face, near your eyes.

Chapter Seven: Caring for your Alaskan Klee Kai

4. Give the command, "Focus" or "Watch."

5. When he glances in your eyes, praise and then give the treat.

6. Repeat until you do not need to bait him to focus with a treat.

f) "Drop It!"

"Drop it" can be a life saving command since it will get your Alaskan Klee Kai to drop anything that you do not want them to have. "Drop it" is quite easy to teach but you need to set your dog up for the exercise or wait for him to have something that you need to take. To teach "drop it." do the following:

1. Have the dog grab something with his mouth. Playing fetch is a great way to encourage this.

2. Once he has something in his mouth, grab it with one hand. In the other, have a treat.

3. Give the command, "drop it."

4. Place the treat near his nose so he can smell it. He should drop the item.

5. If he does, praise and treat.

6. If he does not, you can place your hand over his nose. This will cause him to drop it as it is difficult to breath and uncomfortable for the dog.

7. When he drops the item, act like he did it without being forced; praise and treat.

g) "Leave It!"

"Leave it." like "drop it." is another command that could save your dog's life. Teaching them to leave things alone on the ground will keep them from eating dangerous items on walks. To teach "leave it." you want to work in stages. Start by leaving things in your hands and then moving up to leaving things on the ground.

1. Place a treat in your hand and close your fist.

2. Hold it in front of your dog and give the command, "leave it."

3. Allow him to sniff the treat and try to get at it but ignore him when he is doing this.

4. Once he stops, even for a second, praise the dog and give him a treat with your other hand. Do not give the treat from the hand you told him to leave.

5. Repeat.

6. Increase the difficulty as your dog gets better with the command. Place the treat on your open hand, then on the ground under your cupped hand, and then on the ground without your hand covering. Always treat the dog when he visibly leaves the treat when you give the command.

h) Housetraining

The final section on training that I want to cover is housetraining. Although we focus on the dog learning to not go inside the house, it is more about training the owner to watch the puppy. The simple fact of housetraining is that a puppy needs to go to the bathroom every few hours, and

Chapter Seven: Caring for your Alaskan Klee Kai

---

accidents often happen because owners are not properly watching the dog.

For that reason, it is important to really follow the rules of housetraining. If you follow them, you will find your Alaskan Klee Kai is housetrained very quickly.

Rule Number 1: Keep Watch on your Puppy

The first rule with housetraining is to watch your puppy. Generally, the puppy will give cues, such as sniffing around, going to squat, that will indicate he has to go to the bathroom.

If you are unable to watch your puppy, place him in a crate or somewhere secure where there is non-porous flooring. Generally, puppies will not soil their bed so if you keep your Alaskan Klee Kai in his bed when you cannot watch him, he will be less likely to have an accident.

Rule Number 2: Understand when your Puppy has to Go

Another important rule is to understand when your puppy has to go to the bathroom. In general, puppies will have to go to the bathroom after the following:

- 5 to 20 minutes after eating or drinking;
- When they first wake up;
- After a play period; and
- Every 30 to 45 minutes when awake

By following this rule and taking your puppy out after each of these common times for them to go to the bathroom, you should be able to prevent 95% of the accidents.

Chapter Seven: Caring for your Alaskan Klee Kai

Rule Number 3: Don't Scold

I have seen it time and time again, an upset dog owner sees their Alaskan Klee Kai squatting and peeing on the carpet, they yell and start scolding the puppy...only to have the puppy pee again. Nothing positive is accomplished with scolding a puppy who pees in the house.

Instead, when an accident happens, clap your hands or say "No" if the dog is in the middle of going to the bathroom. This will break the action and often puppies will stop urinating mid-stream.

As soon as he stops, scoop him up and take him immediately outside. Once he starts again, praise him.

When you are cleaning up the area, place the puppy in his crate and then clean it up so he cannot see it.

One thing that I want to mention is that you should not train with puppy pads unless there is some reason, such as limited mobility. Puppy pads can have the adverse effect of teaching the puppy it is okay to go to the bathroom inside.

Rule Number Four: Be Persistent

Although it may seem like you are outside all the time, it is important to be persistent. Take your Alaskan Klee Kai outside and wait 10 to 15 minutes or until he has gone to the bathroom.

If he has not gone to the bathroom after the allotted time, pick him up and place him in his crate. Do not scold or tell him he is bad, simply place him in his crate. Wait about 5 to 10 minutes and then take him outside again.

Chapter Seven: Caring for your Alaskan Klee Kai

Repeat the process until he has gone to the bathroom. The reason why you are placing him in his crate is to prevent him coming inside and immediately going to the bathroom.

Rule Number Five: Praise, Praise and more Praise

Finally, make sure you praise your dog. I like to wait until he squats outside and starts going to the bathroom, then the entire time he is going, I say, "Good dog, go do your business." "Do your business" becomes a command for the dog and while the dog will not defecate on command, when you say, "Do your business." the dog will know that now isn't the time to sniff around and play and he will go to the washroom.

For dogs that are more difficult to train, I will treat the dog whenever he goes outside. This will quickly teach him that going to the bathroom outside is a very good thing.

And those are the basics of training your Alaskan Klee Kai. Remember that training lasts the life of your dog and you should spend time every day training him, even when he is fully trained.

Chapter 8: Feeding your Alaskan Klee Kai

Chapter Eight: Feeding your Alaskan Klee Kai

Although feeding your Alaskan Klee Kai does not have to be any more complicated than simply pouring out the dog food, I always recommend that owners take the time to understand feeding. Providing your dog with the best possible diet goes a long way in boosting his health.

In addition, avoiding foods with a lot of fillers and chemicals by buying high quality foods will help reduce the risk of some health problems.

1. Types of Food

When we are looking at feeding our Alaskan Klee Kai, it is important to look at the various foods that you can offer your dog. There are hundreds of different dog food brands out there so making the choice can be a little overwhelming.

To get started, I always recommend a grain free food. Grains, such as corn, are often used as fillers and many dogs are allergic to them. They offer no nutritional value and are simply empty calories. In addition, they go through the dog without being digested so the rule of thumb is more grains equals more poop.

Another suggestion I make is to use the food the breeder is using, unless they are feeding a substandard food. Switching the food quickly can lead to stomach upset for your puppy and a lot of messes to clean up.

There are actually four types of food to choose from. In terms of the right brand, it comes down to research.

Food Type Number One: Dry Food

The most common and least expensive food that you can give your dog is dry food. This includes pellets, flaked

Chapter Eight: Feeding your Alaskan Klee Kai

food, mixes, biscuits and kibbles. Dry is very popular and it does have some benefits, such as keeping teeth clean.

They have all the nutritional values as other foods but they do not have a high moisture level. Dry food can go stale but it can sit in a bowl without going bad through the day.

Food Type Number Two: Wet Food

Wet food is food that usually comes in a can and has the consistency of canned fish or chili. It has a very high moisture level and is usually higher in calories than dry food. It can be more expensive than dry food but you tend to feed less so it balances out.

I do not recommend wet food for Alaskan Klee Kai for several reasons. First, wet food can lead to diarrhea. Secondly, it does not clean the teeth and thirdly, it can be hard to preserve. Instead, I recommend it as a gravy to make dry food more palatable, but remember to adjust the amount of dry food you are using if you mix in wet. Otherwise, your dog may become overweight.

Food Type Number Three: Semi-moist Food

Semi-moist food comes in small satchels and usually has a kibble like shape in a meaty gravy. Like wet food, it is usually more expensive than dry but again, it has higher calories per serving. It is usually done as a treat for a dog since it is quite expensive.

Like wet food, it works well when you blend it with dry food but I wouldn't recommend it as the only food you feed your dog.

Chapter Eight: Feeding your Alaskan Klee Kai

Food Type Number Four: Raw/Homemade Food

The final type of food that you can give your dog is raw food or a homemade diet. Raw has a lot of benefits including giving your dog high quality nutrients and a lot of variety. You can tailor the food to your individual Alaskan Klee Kai's needs and you can change it slightly to add in fruits and vegetables.

In addition to the variety, dogs tend to digest more of the raw diet than they do with the dry kibble so it means less waste to be picked up. Dogs love the taste, and the diet can be modified to suit allergies and finicky eaters, especially sensitive older dogs.

The downside to raw is that there can be some risk of salmonella and other bacterial poisoning if the food is not properly made or stored. In addition, if you are creating the recipes yourself, you could end up with nutritional deficiencies in your Alaskan Klee Kai.

Chapter Eight: Feeding your Alaskan Klee Kai

It is important to do the research before feeding any type of food. Make sure that it is complete, of a good quality and free of chemicals. If you do that, you will increase the health of your pet.

3. Feeding your Alaskan Klee Kai

Feeding your Alaskan Klee Kai can be quite easy and simple. It is important to note that how you feed, when you feed and how much you feed will vary depending on the individual dog and the food that you are using.

a) When to Feed

When to feed should be based on the age of your dog and also on your schedule. With new Alaskan Klee Kai puppy owners, I recommend that you feed your puppy three times a day. Once in the morning, once around lunch time and once in the evening.

As your puppy grows, you can begin to leave out the lunch feeding and move to two meals a day. Never feed only one meal a day. One meal can cause the dog to have some stomach problems and the dog may not eat as much in one sitting.

In addition to feeding twice a day, I recommend that you feed the dog when you first wake up in the morning. While your Alaskan Klee Kai is eating, get ready for your day and then he will be ready to go outside right before you leave for the day.

In the evening, feed him when you get home from work, or around dinner time, and he will have gone outside before bedtime. And that is really all there is to know about timing.

Chapter Eight: Feeding your Alaskan Klee Kai

b) How much to Feed

The amount of food depends on the age of your dog, how active the dog is and the type of food you are feeding. High quality dog foods require less food while low quality requires more, so your dog can reach the necessary caloric intake. With feeding, it is important to look at the weight of your dog, as well as his energy level and age.

To do this, we are looking at the resting energy requirements. What this means is how many calories is the dog burning when at rest. From there, we can begin to adjust the amount of food, or calories that we need to feed the dog.

Determining your dog's resting energy requirements is simple. Take your dog's weight in kilograms and multiply it by 30. Then add 70. So if you have a 23 pound Alaskan Klee Kai, you would divide 23 by 2.2 for a total of 10.45 or 10.5 if we round up. Multiply 10.5 by 30 for 315 and then add 70 for a total of 385 calories per day. Most dog food bags have the calorie amount for every half cup or cup so you simply divide the calories needed by the calories provided.

For instance, Purina Dog Chow Complete Nutrition has 430 calories for every cup of dog food. So dividing 430 by 385 means that the dog would need slightly more than 3/4 cups of food to meet his caloric intake needs.

The main hitch with this equation is that it is looking at the resting energy requirements and as you know, Alaskan Klee Kai are very active little dogs. When we are taking into account the activity levels and age of your dog, we want to take the resting energy requirements and multiply it by a set number, which is outlined in the chart below.

Chapter Eight: Feeding your Alaskan Klee Kai

Activity Level/Age	Multiplier for Resting Energy Requirements
Weaning to 4 months	X 3.0
4 months to adult	X 2.0
Lactating female	X 4.8
Pregnant female day 1 to 42	X 1.8
Pregnant female day 42 to whelping	X 3.0
Adult Dog neutered/spayed with normal activity	X 1.6
Adult Dog intact with normal activity	X 1.8
Adult Dog with light activity	X 2.0
Adult Dog with moderate activity	X 3.0
Adult Dog with heavy activity	X 4.8
Adult Dog needing weight loss	X 1.0

As you can see, the daily calories can change depending on the individual dog. So if the same Alaskan Klee Kai from above, who needs 385 calories per day, was a female with nursing puppies, her calories for the day should be 1848 or slightly more than 4 cups of Purina dog chow.

When we are looking at raw feeding, the amounts are slightly different. In addition, it is difficult to determine the calories as it will be different with the feed you are giving. A pound of beef with 30% blend of organ, meat and bone has about 2600 calories in it, so the Alaskan Klee Kai that weighs 23 pounds only needs about 0.2 pounds of such food per day. The reason for this is because the multiplier

Chapter Eight: Feeding your Alaskan Klee Kai

for the resting energy requirements is higher when feeding raw, which is outlined in the chart below.

Activity Level/Age	Multiplier for Resting Energy Requirements
Weaning to 4 months	X 6.0
4 months to adult	X 4.0
Lactating female	X 8.0
Pregnant female day 1 to 42	X 4.0
Pregnant female day 42 to whelping	X 6.0
Adult Dog neutered/spayed with normal activity	X 2.0
Adult Dog intact with normal activity	X 2.5
Adult Dog with light activity	X 3.0
Adult Dog with moderate activity	X 3.5
Adult Dog with heavy activity	X 4.0
Adult Dog needing weight loss	X 1.5

c) How to Feed

When we talk about how to feed, it is not just putting the food into a bowl. The question is whether to free feed or not. Free feeding means to fill your dog's dish and allow him access to it constantly.

While it seems like a great idea, I strongly recommend against it. Free feeding can lead to many problems such as aggression, obesity and even weight loss if you have other pets in the home that are eating all the food.

Chapter Eight: Feeding your Alaskan Klee Kai

Instead of free feeding, make set times for feeding. Pour the desired amount into the bowl and then give the dog 20 minutes to finish it. If the dog does not finish it, pick it up and save the food for his next meal time.

If your dog does not eat, he will eventually do so (unless something is medically wrong). Feeding in this manner will allow you to keep track of his calorie intake and also prevent food bowl aggression.

4. Watering your Alaskan Klee Kai

An Alaskan Klee Kai should be offered water throughout the day. They will drink more water during the hot summer months than during the winter. Be generous with the water.

Water should be cool but be careful with ice cold water. Too much ice cold water can lead to tummy problems with your Alaskan Klee Kai.

When it comes to the amount of water I recommend and how to present it, I make suggestions according to age. Young puppies that are not fully housetrained should only be offered water at set times. This will help reduce the amount of times the puppy has to go to the washroom. Another rule with young dogs is to pick up the water dish about 2 to 4 hours before you go to bed.

With adult dogs, or housetrained dogs, you can leave the water down all the time for them.

To determine if your dog has enough water in the day, you should follow the rule of weight. In general, you should give your dog one ounce of water for every pound of dog, or 66ml for every kilogram of dog.

Chapter Eight: Feeding your Alaskan Klee Kai

With that equation in mind, if you own a standard Alaskan Klee Kai that weighs 23 pounds (10kg), then you should give the dog at least 23 ounces (660ml or 3 cups) of water, more if it is a warm day.

5. Treats for your Alaskan Klee Kai

Walk through a pet store and you will see that there are hundreds of different dog treats to choose from. Really, getting a treat for your Alaskan Klee Kai is as simple as walking into a store. But I want to stress that you should consider a few things before reaching for a treat.

The first thing is that treats are just that—treats. You should never just feed the treats without thinking about the added calories. Yes, even Alaskan Klee Kai need to watch their waistline and feeding treats freely can lead to obesity in your dog.

A general rule of thumb to follow with treats is to only allow them to take up 10% of your dog's daily calories. In

Chapter Eight: Feeding your Alaskan Klee Kai

addition, always calculate the calories into their daily intake.

When you are selecting treats for your dogs, follow these rules:

Tip Number One: Avoid Table Scraps

While it can be tempting to feed your dog from the table, you should avoid it. The main reason is that a lot of human food contains additives that can be harmful to your Alaskan Klee Kai. Read the next section on foods to avoid for more information.

Tip Number Two: Choose Natural Ingredients

When you are purchasing treats from the store, read the ingredients label. Only choose foods that have natural ingredients and avoid foods with processed ingredients. Another rule of thumb is to avoid anything with a chemical name as most chemicals in dog food have been linked to cancer.

Tip Number Three: Don't Buy Products Made in China

Although most of the products are safe for your dog, it is important to remember that products made in China do not have all the safety standards of other countries. Many products are made with dangerous chemicals that have been linked to liver disease, cancer and even resulted in death.

Tip Number Four: Use Fresh Foods

While we often think of dog treats as bones or manufactured foods, it can be as simple as giving your dog a carrot. In fact, many fruits and vegetables are safe for

Chapter Eight: Feeding your Alaskan Klee Kai

your Alaskan Klee Kai and make an excellent treat for your dog.

Tip Number Five: Think of Health Benefits

Finally, when you are choosing your treats, think of health options. Many treats have supplements in them that will help prevent arthritis, boost their immune system and a range of other benefits so I recommend checking the ingredients list to check for healthy vitamins and to make sure there are no chemicals in the food.

With those tips in mind, I close this section off with a list of healthy snack choices for your Alaskan Klee Kai.

Apples: remove seeds	Kale
Applesauce	Lemons
Apricots: remove pits	Marrow Bones
Baby food: all-natural, make sure it is free of salt	Mint
Bananas	Nectarines: remove pits
Beef: raw and cooked	Oatmeal
Beets	Organ meats: heart, liver, kidney, etc.
Blackberries	Pasta: cooked
Blueberries	Peaches: remove pits
Bran cereal	Peanut butter
Bread: avoid nut breads and raison bread	Pears
Broccoli: safe when fed raw	Peas

Chapter Eight: Feeding your Alaskan Klee Kai

Brussels Sprouts	Pineapple
Cantaloupe	Plums: remove pits
Carrots	Pumpkin
Cauliflower: safe when fed raw	Rice: cooked only
Celery	Rice cakes
Cheerios cereal	Salmon
Cheese: cheddar is safe	Spinach
Chicken: remove bones if cooked	Squash
Corn: safe off the cob	Strawberries
Cottage cheese	Sweet potatoes
Cranberries	Tomatoes
Cream cheese	Training treats
Cucumbers	Tuna
Dog Cookies: homemade and store bought	Turkey: cooked with bones removed
Eggs: when cooked	Watermelon
Flax seed	Yogurt
Green beans	Zucchini
Honey	

6. Foods to Avoid

I have outlined a diet that you should feed to your Alaskan Klee Kai. It is also important to go over foods that you should never feed them. While some foods are safe for people, there are a range of foods that can have

Chapter Eight: Feeding your Alaskan Klee Kai

catastrophic effects on your Alaskan Klee Kai if you feed them to him.

Below is a chart that goes over foods you should avoid giving to your dog.

Foods to Avoid	Reasons to Avoid
Alcohol	Can lead to a coma and/or death
Apple Seeds	Seeds contain cyanide and can lead to death.
Artificial Sweetener	Can cause low blood sugar, vomiting, collapse and liver failure.
Avocado	May cause vomiting and diarrhea
Broccoli	When cooked, it can cause gas, which can lead to bloating. Safe when it is raw.
Cat Food	While not harmful, too much cat food can lead to health problems due to the high protein and fat content.
Cauliflower	When cooked, it can cause gas, which can lead to bloating. Safe when it is raw.
Chocolate	Contains caffeine and can lead to vomiting and diarrhea. Can lead to death if too much is consumed.
Chicken	Cooked chicken has bones that can splinter, which can lead to an obstruction or laceration in the digestive system.
Citrus	May cause vomiting.
Citrus Oil	May cause vomiting.
Coffee	Contains caffeine and can lead to vomiting and diarrhea. Can lead to death if too much is consumed.

Chapter Eight: Feeding your Alaskan Klee Kai

Currants	Can cause kidney damage and death.
Fat Trimmings	High fat levels can lead to pancreatitis.
Fish	Bones can lacerate the digestive system. In addition, if fed a fish exclusive diet, it can lead to vitamin B deficiency, which can cause seizures and death. Fish in dog food is fine as long as other nutrients are in the ingredients list. Fish skin is also a nutritious treat.
Garlic	Can cause anemia.
Grapes	Can cause kidney damage and death.
Grape Seed Oil	Can cause kidney damage and death.
Gum	Can cause blockages and contains Xylitol, which can damage the liver.
Hops	Can cause increased heart rate, fever, seizures and sometimes, death.
Human Vitamins	Can damage a dog's liver, kidneys and digestive system.
Macadamia Nuts	Toxin in the nuts can cause seizures and death.
Milk	Along with other dairy products, can cause diarrhea.
Mushrooms	Can cause shock, shut down multiple body systems and can lead to death.
Onions	Can cause anemia.
Persimmons	The seeds lead to intestinal obstructions.
Peaches	The flesh of the peach is fine, however, be sure to remove the pit or it can cause an obstruction.

Chapter Eight: Feeding your Alaskan Klee Kai

Pork	Has bones that will splinter, which can lead to an obstruction or laceration in the digestive system.
Plums	The flesh of the plum is fine, however, be sure to remove the pit or it can cause an obstruction.
Raisins	Can cause kidney damage and death.
Raw Eggs	Can cause skin and coat problems since it decreases the absorption of biotin.
Rhubarb Leaves	Poisonous, can affect the urinary tract system, digestive system and nervous system.
Salt	Can lead to vomiting, diarrhea, dehydration and seizures. Large quantities can lead to death.
Sugar	Leads to obesity and has been linked to canine diabetes.
Tea	Contains caffeine and can lead to vomiting and diarrhea. Can lead to death if too much is consumed.
Tomato Greens/Plant	Can cause heart problems in dogs.
Turkey	Cooked turkey has bones that will splinter, which can lead to an obstruction or laceration in the digestive system.
Yeast	Can cause pain, gas and can even cause a rupture in the digestive system, which can result in death.

Chapter 9: Socializing and Training your Alaskan Klee Kai

Chapter Nine: Socializing and Training your Alaskan Klee Kai

One important aspect of owning an Alaskan Klee Kai is to properly train and socialize your puppy and your dog. While many people think of socializing and training as something you do with a puppy, it is actually important to do both throughout the life of your Alaskan Klee Kai.

Even a perfectly trained dog will slip into some bad habits and with spending a few minutes a day doing training, you can avoid this from happening.

In this chapter, I will take you through the key points on socializing and training your Alaskan Klee Kai. I want to stress that this chapter, in no way, replaces the advice and training by a professional dog trainer. I recommend that you attend puppy socialization as well as obedience classes.

1. Socializing your Alaskan Klee Kai

As I have mentioned, socializing your Alaskan Klee Kai is an important step in developing a well-rounded dog. In many ways, socialization begins the moment the puppies are born. There are many things that your breeder will do that will establish the puppies' socialization.

Generally, when we think of socialization, we think of it in terms of being social with others. This can be with people, other dogs or children. While being 'social' is one important aspect of socializing, it is just that, one aspect.

Instead of focusing socialization on one area, you should focus on the complete dog. Socialize the dog to a range of stimuli and this will help create a mentally balanced dog that does not frighten easily.

Chapter Nine: Socializing and Training your Alaskan Klee Kai

a) What is Socialization?

By definition, socialization means having the skills to be part of society. In a dog's world, socialization leads to a dog being a productive part of their surroundings. Dogs should be taught to accept things they will see on a day to day basis. In addition, they should accept people and other animals.

Socialization is when we expose a puppy and/or dog to a host of different stimuli and encourage them to accept or not even notice that stimuli.

The process of socialization is very important since dogs that are not properly socialized can become timid and fearful. In addition, they can become aggressive to animals, other dogs and to people.

b) When Should I Socialize?

I am a firm believer in socialization being a lifelong process and that socialization should begin as soon as dogs come home. Socialization outside the home should start at around 12-weeks-old when they have been properly vaccinated.

The key period of socialization is between the ages of 12 weeks to 5 months old. During that time, your Alaskan Klee Kai will go through various developmental milestones, which will go smoothly if socialization is done properly.

In addition to these periods, you should be aware that puppies will go through fear periods. Your confident Alaskan Klee Kai may suddenly become a very fearful Klee Kai almost overnight. This is normal and you simply continue socializing your puppy as you normally would.

Chapter Nine: Socializing and Training your Alaskan Klee Kai

Fear periods in dogs differ depending on the breed but in the Alaskan Klee Kai, you should expect it to be between 5 to 7 months old and then, possibly, again around 16 to 18 months of age.

c) How do I Socialize?

Socialization is done a bit at a time and it is important to follow a few rules to help keep socialization positive. Remember that you want your Alaskan Klee Kai to not see other dogs as negative. If it is negative, then the dog will have more problems than if he was not socialized at all.

Rule Number One: Make the Socialization Fun

Always make sure that every socialization time that he has is a fun one. Let the puppy play around the stimuli so that he can learn that it is not a negative thing. Stimuli would typically include; new streets, new dogs, and different noises.

Rule Number Two: Let It Be at His Pace

Although our first response is to nudge our puppy closer to the thing we are socializing him to, it is important to allow

Chapter Nine: Socializing and Training your Alaskan Klee Kai

your Alaskan Klee Kai to approach the object at his own pace.

It may take several socialization experiences before the puppy will go and approach the new item but you should take your time. Never force the experience or push the dog towards the stimuli.

Rule Number Three: Give your Alaskan Klee Kai Space

Sit close to your Alaskan Klee Kai so you can be a reassurance to him but also let him have space. You want him to feel like he can retreat and approach the stimuli as he likes. If he feels cornered or trapped, it will make the socialization a negative experience.

When it comes to people, use the same rule. Have them sit away from the puppy and then allow the puppy to go and greet them.

Rule Number Four: Mix it up

Another important rule is to mix up the socialization. Your Alaskan Klee Kai may have no problem with dogs when he is in his home but outside of his home may be a different story. Take the time to set up socialization outside of the house and in the house. Take him to lots of places, introduce him to the same things you introduced in the home, within reason—for instance, you are not as likely to run into a vacuum on the street.

Do the reverse when he is at home. Often, people forget the importance of inviting others over so the Alaskan Klee Kai can learn to accept things both in his house and outside of it. Remember, the Alaskan Klee Kai can be very territorial so you want to make visitors an accepted norm.

Chapter Nine: Socializing and Training your Alaskan Klee Kai

Rule Number Five: Use Reinforcement

Finally, use rewards for reinforcement when you are socializing your puppy. Things like treats, verbal encouragement and praise will help your Alaskan Klee Kai be successful with a socialization exercise.

One word of caution with rewards is to never reward your dog when he is scared. This includes babying the dog when he is frightened or giving a negative reinforcement when he does not socialize the way you want him to.

Babying will only let your puppy know that it is okay to be scared and correction or negative reinforcement will make the Alaskan Klee Kai more fearful than he already is.

d) What Should I Socialize to?

The final point that I want to make on socialization is what you should socialize to. While everyone has different living circumstances that will change your socialization stimuli, there are a number of stimuli that you should do, regardless. Below is a checklist to get you started with socializing your Alaskan Klee Kai.

Stimuli	X	Stimuli	X
Men: Bearded and clean-shaven		Balls of various size	
Women		Mirrors	
Children: Boys and Girls		Baby strollers	
Toddlers: Boys and Girls		Grocery carts	
Babies: Boys and Girls		Mirrors	
People with glasses		Brooms	

Chapter Nine: Socializing and Training your Alaskan Klee Kai

People with crutches		Dusters	
People with canes		Vacuum cleaners	
People in wheelchairs		Wind	
Slouched people		Flags	
People with walkers		Tents	
Shuffling people		Flashlights	
Large crowds		Children's Toys	
Small crowds		Television	
People on roller blades		Plastic bags	
People of various shapes and sizes: tall, thin, heavy, short, etc.		Umbrellas	
People with sunglasses		Balloons	
People who are exercising		Skateboards	
People on bikes		Children playing	
Costumes		Hammering	
Bald people		Construction equipment	
Big dogs		Lawn mowers	
Little dogs		Scooters	
Farm animals		Buses	
Puppies		Trains	
Small Rodent/non canine		Sirens	
Birds		Ceiling fans	
Lizards		Garage doors	
Escalators		Dremel tools	

Chapter Nine: Socializing and Training your Alaskan Klee Kai

Cars: Both while walking and riding in them		Fireworks	
Sliding doors		Cheering	
Planes (optional)		Yelling	
Elevators		Radios	
Escalators		Storms	
Alarms		Loud noises	
Singing		Visiting the vet	
Grooming		Getting nails cut	
Being crated		Being picked up	
Having all body parts touched		Leash	
Collar		Harnesses	

As you can see, there is a lot to socialize your Alaskan Klee Kai to and these only touch on some of the more common stimuli.

2. Training your Alaskan Klee Kai

Before we get into training your Alaskan Klee Kai, I want to stress the importance of going to a professional trainer. While a lot of training can be done at home, puppy kindergarten and obedience training will help prevent mistakes and will offer ample socialization to your puppy.

Training an Alaskan Klee Kai can be very easy if you follow the proper type of training. This is a breed that is very intelligent so they can learn a command very quickly. In addition, the Alaskan Klee Kai is usually eager to please. What this means is that the breed wants to make

Chapter Nine: Socializing and Training your Alaskan Klee Kai

their owners happy so they will do things that are asked of them.

That being said, an Alaskan Klee Kai does have a strong mind and he will quickly rule the home if he finds leadership is lacking. For that reason, the type of training that you should use is the Alpha dog training.

Alpha dog training is when you establish yourself as the top of the pack. As pack leader, you have to provide the rules and necessities of life for the pack. If you do not have strong leadership and cannot be firm and consistent with rules, then you should not own an Alaskan Klee Kai.

In addition to establishing yourself as pack leader, it is important to establish the hierarchy in your family for the Klee Kai, children above the dog and so on. With other animals, establish rules but let them establish their pack leadership. Forcing a dominant dog to be submissive to an animal that is not dominant enough to be a leader can cause real problems.

Chapter Nine: Socializing and Training your Alaskan Klee Kai

Alpha training does not involve harsh correction. Alpha training involves positive reinforcement, where you use treats to get a dog to learn a command.

However, alpha training is also about establishing rules and maintaining them. It is about providing for the needs of your dog and not babying the animal. Babying an Alaskan Klee Kai can cause a lot of problems, including small dog syndrome, which is linked to aggression, problem barking and destructive behaviors.

The Alaskan Klee Kai requires rules and it is important to be consistent with them. Before you bring the puppy home, think of the rules that you want to have in your house. If you are fine with dogs on the furniture, allow it. If not, do not allow it from the very moment puppy comes home. It may not seem like a big deal but it will confuse your Alaskan Klee Kai when you finally tell him to stay off.

One thing that I teach my dogs early on is that they do not come on the furniture without permission. For the first 6 months, they are told off and placed on the floor whenever they climb up. After 6 months of age, I slowly allow them up but only when I invite them. If you follow this, you will quickly find your Alaskan Klee Kai being extremely polite and finding ways to ask for permission.

When training your Alaskan Klee Kai, be sure to follow these rules:

Rule Number One: Be First

When it comes to establishing yourself as a pack leader, make sure that you are always the first. Go through doors before your Alaskan Klee Kai, eat first, go downstairs first and so on.

Chapter Nine: Socializing and Training your Alaskan Klee Kai

Rule Number Two: Make him Work

Regardless of whether you are giving him food, a treat or praise, you want him to work for it. Always give your Alaskan Klee Kai a command, such as "sit" and "wait" at dinner time, before you give him some form of reward. This will teach him that he needs to work for things and will also help with manners so he is not jumping at things.

Rule Number Three: Be the Initiator

Playing, cuddling, and any type of attention should be done with you initiating it. Pick up toys, although you can leave out a few to combat chewing, and bring them out for play sessions.

Do not give in if he brings the toys to you and is pushy to get you to play. In addition, do not pay attention to your Alaskan Klee Kai if he is jumping or biting at you to get attention. Instead, ignore him until he is sitting politely and then give him the attention. Again, this goes back to working for things since sitting nicely is working.

Rule Number Four: Give your Alaskan Klee Kai his own Space

While it can be tempting to keep your dog with you at all times, make sure that you give him his own space as well. I recommend crate training as it keeps puppies from chewing when you are not home.

This area will give him a chance to take a break when the house is too busy or when he is tired. In addition, it will be a safe place for him and that will help establish roles in your home. Not only will he feel secure with your leadership but also with his role in the house.

Chapter Nine: Socializing and Training your Alaskan Klee Kai

Rule Number Five: Always have Access to his Food

Finally, always make sure that you have access to the food dish. When he is a puppy, take the time to have your hands in his dish and also make sure that you feed him a few handfuls.

If your Alaskan Klee Kai becomes too pushy when you have your hand in his dish, lift the dish up and feed him by hand only until he relaxes. You want to make it clear that the food dish belongs to you and he is simply allowed to eat from it.

You also want to teach him that the food will be given back to him when he behaves. Have everyone in the house do the food dish exercise. While it will help with establishing leadership, it will also help prevent food guarding or aggression.

In the end, when you are training your Alaskan Klee Kai, be consistent and firm and make it fun. If you do that, and provide strong leadership, you will find your Alaskan Klee Kai is both easy and a joy to train.

Chapter 10: Alaskan Klee Kai Health

Chapter Ten: Alaskan Klee Kai Health

Alaskan Klee Kai are considered to be a vigorous breed with very few health problems. That being said, there are a number of diseases that affect the Alaskan Klee Kai and it is important to make sure that you purchase a dog from a reputable breeder.

Generally, a reputable breeder will have the parents' health tested before they breed them. Important tests for the Alaskan Klee Kai are:

- Eyes Certified;
- Factor VII Status;
- OFA Thyroid;
- OFA Cardiac; and
- OFA Knees.

By purchasing from a breeder who health tests his or her lines, you are less likely to run into the hereditary illnesses that can affect the breed.

However, even with the best screening, some diseases can manifest themselves, and this chapter is about identifying illnesses in your dog as well as the common health problems of Alaskan Klee Kai.

1. Signs of Illness

Although signs of illness may differ depending on the disease or illness affecting a dog, there are some general signs that you should look out for. When your Alaskan Klee Kai has any of these symptoms, it is important to seek veterinarian care.

One thing that I should stress is that with any breed, including the Alaskan Klee Kai is that illnesses often come

Chapter Ten: Alaskan Klee Kai Health

on suddenly and it is very easy for a dog to go quickly from healthy to gravely ill. Make sure you monitor your dogs frequently and carry out a daily health check on your Alaskan Klee Kai.

Symptoms that your dog may be sick are:

Bad Breath

Bad breath is often a sign of some oral problem but it can also be a sign of other diseases. If the Klee Kai has bad breath, and there is no root cause for it that you can see, schedule an appointment with your vet.

Drooling

Alaskan Klee Kai are not known as a breed that drools. Instead, they are fairly dry mouthed so a lot of drooling may indicate oral health issues or even stomach problems.

Chapter Ten: Alaskan Klee Kai Health

Loss of Appetite

Loss of appetite is often one of the first indicators that something is wrong with your Alaskan Klee Kai. With loss of appetite, it is very important to look at the pattern of eating. If your dog is usually a picky eater, missing the occasional meal should not give rise to concerns.

In addition, if you have a female that has not been spayed, she may stop eating around her heat cycles. Pregnancy can also lead to a dog eating somewhat less.

The biggest concern is when your dog is not eating for more than 24 hours, especially if other symptoms are seen.

Excessive Thirst

Outside of days with hot weather, if your Alaskan Klee Kai seems to be drinking large amounts of water, then it could be an indication of disease or dehydration. In general, an Alaskan Klee Kai should drink about an ounce of water for every pound of dog. <u>So a 20 pound Alaskan Klee Kai should have 20 ounces (2.5 cups) of water every day.</u>

Changes in Urination

Changes in the color of urine as well as the frequency of urination can indicate a health problem. It is important to note that an increase in urination can be linked to some illnesses while difficulty urinating can indicate other ones.

If you spot blood in the urine, contact your vet immediately.

Chapter Ten: Alaskan Klee Kai Health

Skin Problems

The skin of the Alaskan Klee Kai should be smooth and pink or black color. If the skin is bright red or flaking, then it could indicate a health problem.

In addition, if the dog is scratching a lot, it could have fleas, some type of mite, or allergies. Make sure you check off all the reasons for the skin problems.

Lethargy

Alaskan Klee Kai are active dogs with ample energy. For that reason, any lethargy can be cause for concern. Like changes in appetite, make sure that you identify any reasons why your dog is tired, such as being over exercised. If there are no apparent reasons, contact your vet.

Gum Problems

Although gum problems indicate teeth or gum disease, they can actually be linked to other serious diseases that can affect your Alaskan Klee Kai. Things to look for are:

- ***Swollen Gums:*** Swollen gums, when accompanied by bad breath, can indicate gum disease or other oral problems.

- ***Bright Red Gums:*** When a Klee Kai's gums are bright red, it could be an indication that the dog is fighting an infection. Exposure to toxins is another reason for bright red gums.

- ***Blue Gums:*** Blue gums indicate that the Alaskan Klee Kai is lacking oxygen for some reason. Seek immediate veterinarian care.

Chapter Ten: Alaskan Klee Kai Health

- ***Purple Gums:*** Purple gums are often seen when a dog has gone into shock or there is a problem with his blood circulation. What has happened before you notice the purple gums in your Alaskan Klee Kai will indicate whether the dog is in shock or not.

- ***Grey Gums:*** The same as purple gums, when grey gums are seen in an Alaskan Klee Kai, it can indicate either poor blood circulation or shock.

- ***Pale Pink:*** Pale pink gums can be an indication of anemia in the Alaskan Klee Kai.

- ***White Gums:*** Finally, white gums can be an indication of a loss of blood. This loss can be either externally or internally so contact your vet immediately.

As you can see, gums are one of the primary indicators of illness in dogs. If your dog does not have pink gums, but has black instead, you can check his health by looking at the pink portion of his lower eyelid.

Changes in Weight

This is something that is not always easy to follow since it means relying on charting his weight, but if you notice unexpected weight loss or weight gain in your Alaskan Klee Kai, there could be an underlying condition.

Stiffness of Limbs

As a spry little dog, an Alaskan Klee Kai does not usually have stiffness in his limbs. While old age can create some stiffness, there are several diseases that can affect mobility. If you notice he has difficulty in getting up, climbing stairs or walking, there may be an underlying problem.

Chapter Ten: Alaskan Klee Kai Health

Respiratory Problems

Whenever you see excessive sneezing, coughing, labored breathing and panting, take note. It could be nothing but often, respiratory problems are an early indication that there is a health problem.

Runny Eyes or Nose

If you see any discharge or fluid coming out of your Alaskan Klee Kai eyes or nose, keep close watch on his symptoms. This can be linked to several conditions including respiratory illnesses.

Vomiting and Gagging

Dogs will gag and vomit without being ill, but if you see repeated vomiting or the dog has a bowed look and is continually gagging, seek medical help. Vomiting and gagging can be a sign of allergies or could indicate a life threatening disease.

Fluctuations in Temperature

Finally, if you suspect that your Alaskan Klee Kai's health is compromised, it is important to check your dog's temperature. High temperatures can be a symptom of a serious disease. A temperature below normal could indicate other problems such as shock.

Check the temperature with a rectal thermometer or an ear thermometer. Make sure that the Alaskan Klee Kai's temperature is between the following:

- ***Rectal Temperature:*** Rectal temperatures in dogs should be between 100.5 to 102.5°F (38 to 39.2°F)

Chapter Ten: Alaskan Klee Kai Health

- **Ear Temperature:** Ear temperatures in dogs should be between 100 to 103°F (37.7 to 39.4°C).

Human temperatures can fluctuate during the day and so too, do those of dogs, but if you see a temperature of lower or higher than the above, seek veterinarian help. One exception to the rule is in pregnant females. Read the chapter on breeding your Alaskan Klee Kai for further details.

It is important to note that some symptoms, occurring on their own, may not indicate any problem, but if your Alaskan Klee Kai has three or more of the symptoms, you should seek medical care for your dog.

2. Common Health Problems in the Breed

As I have mentioned before, Alaskan Klee Kai are a hardy breed that do not have a lot of known health problems. That being said, with their rising popularity, there has been an increase in some diseases due to poor breeding practices. For that reason, it is important to be aware of these diseases, their symptoms and how they are commonly treated.

a) Factor VII Deficiency

A disease that can be prevented by DNA testing parents and not breeding any dogs testing positive as a carrier for the disease, Factor VII Deficiency is a hereditary disease where clotting does not occur. It is a form of canine hemophilia and the dog may suffer from excessive bleeding after surgery or injury.

Chapter Ten: Alaskan Klee Kai Health

Symptoms

In general, there are very few symptoms that the Alaskan Klee Kai will exhibit. Often, the first sign that a dog has factor VII is during surgery when the dog will continue to lose blood. There are coagulation screening tests that can be done to test the dog for the disorder and it is recommended that you let your vet know about the hereditary factors of this disease for your Alaskan Klee Kai so appropriate testing can be done.

Treatment

There is no known treatment for this disease. There has been some success with recombinant factor VII through a plasma transfusion; however, that treatment has proven to be temporary.

While studies are still new, some researchers have had success with gene therapy but this type of treatment is still in its testing stages.

The best way to treat Factor VII Deficiency is to prevent it. Choose puppies from a litter where both parents have tested clear for the gene.

b) Pyometra

Pyometra is a disease that only affects intact females which means females who have not been spayed. It involves an infection in the uterus. It usually occurs about 4 to 6 weeks after a heat, however, it can be seen at other times as well. It is a very serious infection that needs to be treated quickly or it can turn septic and if left untreated will lead to death.

Chapter Ten: Alaskan Klee Kai Health

Symptoms

Symptoms of pyometra may be very hard to notice at first, however, they will get progressively worse as the illness continues.

Early symptoms include:

- Licking her vulva;
- Frequent urination;
- Excessive thirst; and
- Loss of appetite.

Serious symptoms include:

- Swollen abdomen;
- Dog collapses;
- Yellowish-brown discharge; and
- Vomiting.

Treatment

While some antibiotic treatments have proven successful, dogs that have had pyometra often suffer from fertility issues. For that reason, and due to the seriousness of the disease, the most common form of treatment is spaying the dog and removing her reproductive organs.

c) Juvenile Cataracts

Juvenile cataracts are simply cataracts that occur in puppies. A cataract is a white film that covers the eye and reduces the amount of vision the dogs have. Severe cataracts can lead to blindness. What makes juvenile cataracts different is that it occurs in the young dog where otherwise cataracts occur in older, senior dogs.

Chapter Ten: Alaskan Klee Kai Health

Symptoms

It is important to note that most puppies do not show any signs or symptoms of juvenile cataracts when they are 8 weeks of age. Instead, the condition will often develop around 6 months to 2 years of age. The symptoms of the condition mainly include a white film over the eye.

Treatment

Treatment is done in two ways. The first is with cortisone eye drops, which will dissolve the cataract. If the eye drops do not dissolve the cataract, surgery will be done to the eye where the ocular lens, which is the lens affect, will be removed and replaced with a plastic implant.

Generally, treatment is only done in severe cases as most dogs with juvenile cataracts do not get progressively worse and live a happy life with slightly impaired vision.

d) Patellar Luxation

Patellar luxation is a condition where the dog's kneecap, which is called a patella, is not in its normal position. It has been dislocated, which is why it is commonly called 'floating kneecap.'

The condition can be both hereditary, as it is with the Alaskan Klee Kai, or due to some form of trauma. While it is more commonly seen in females than males, both sexes can have this condition.

When we look at patellar luxation, we are actually looking at four types, which range in severity. These types are:

- *Grade 1:* The kneecap pops out but pops back into place without any intervention.

Chapter Ten: Alaskan Klee Kai Health

- *Grade 2:* The kneecap pops out and while it can pop into place on its own, it usually has to be manipulated to pop back in.
- *Grade 3:* The kneecap spends much of its time sitting outside the correct place without being manually positioned back into place. It will often stay in place for short periods before popping back out.
- *Grade 4:* The kneecap is popped out all of the time and even after being manually put back into position, it will pop out.

Symptoms

There are very few symptoms of patellar luxation since it does not appear to cause the dog pain or discomfort. The only sign is when the dog will have a sudden lameness in the hind leg or an abnormal gait in his hind quarters.

Treatment

Treatment of this condition is usually through surgery where the kneecap will be surgically fastened to remain in place. Treatment is usually only given in severe cases.

e) Cryptorchidism

Cryptorchidism is where one or both testicles do not descend into the scrotum of the animal. Instead, they are retained somewhere in the dog's lower body. This is a condition that is not usually seen until the dog is close to six months of age.

While it may seem like a minor condition, dogs that suffer from cryptorchidism can often develop tumors in their

Chapter Ten: Alaskan Klee Kai Health

testes. In addition, they are 10 times more likely to develop testicular cancer.

Symptoms

There seem to be very few symptoms that owners will notice, except for the lack of testes in the scrotum, or only one testicle.

Occasionally, the dog may have sudden, acute abdominal pain and is usually an indication that the testes have twisted in the dog's body and created a loss of blood to the area.

Treatment

The treatment for cryptorchidism is sterilization of the dog through castration.

f) Liver Shunt

A liver shunt, also known as portosystemic shunt (PSS), involves an abnormality in the vascular anatomy. What this means is that instead of the body sending blood to the liver to have it cleansed of toxins, the liver is bypassed by the shunt and the toxins are released into the body.

It is believed to be a hereditary condition, however, not all dogs are born with it. While some liver shunts are present at birth, many occur later on in life.

Symptoms

It is important to note that the symptoms of a liver shunt will actually come and go. There is no set symptom that will occur all the time. Instead, you should keep track of symptoms and if you see reoccurring symptoms, then it will give some indication that it is a shunt.

Symptoms are:

- Poor growth;
- Interrupted gait;
- Seizures;
- Swaying;
- Head pressing; and
- Poor coat condition.

Treatment

Treatment is often surgery to close or minimize the shunt. Other medical treatment may also be recommended. For both, changes in lifestyle and a diet that is low in protein is recommended. Lactulose supplements have also been used with great success in the past.

g) Heart Murmur

A heart murmur is a condition that is quite common in the Alaskan Klee Kai. It is when there is an extra heart vibration, which is caused by a disturbance in the blood flow. Heart murmurs are graded by severity:

- *Grade I:* There is very little heard, a barely audible heart murmur.
- *Grade II:* The heart murmur is low but it can be picked up with a stethoscope.
- *Grade III:* The heart murmur has an intermediate loudness but is usually only heard on one side of the chest.
- *Grade IV:* A loud heart murmur that can be heard on both sides of the chest.

- **Grade V:** Can be heard very easily throughout the chest and the extra vibration can be felt through the chest wall.
- **Grade VI:** Most severe and the heart murmur can be heard with the stethoscope barely touching the dog. Again, the vibration can be felt through the chest wall.

Symptoms

In lower grade heart murmurs, the symptoms are not noticeable and often, the only reason why owners know that their dog has a heart murmur is through a vet's diagnosis. In more severe cases where the heart murmur is associated with heart disease, you may see the following symptoms:

- Weakness;
- Severe panting;
- Coughing; or
- Collapse after or during exercise.

Treatment

Treatment varies depending on the severity and whether there is an underlying cause for it. A lower-grade heart murmurs is monitored to make sure it does not get worse, while a more severe murmur may be treated by medication, then by diagnosing the underlying condition and changing the diet and lifestyle for the dog.

h) Hypothyroidism

Hypothyroidism is when the thyroid does not produce enough of the hormones T4 and T3. It is a condition that is more commonly seen in dogs that have been fixed.

This condition can be caused by other diseases and conditions or it can be hereditary. While it can affect a dog at any age, it is more commonly seen in dogs between the ages of 4 and 10 years old.

Symptoms

There are many symptoms when a dog has hypothyroidism. These symptoms are:

- Weakness;
- Mental dullness;
- Seizures;
- Hair loss and/or poor hair growth;
- Dull coat;
- Inactivity;
- Lethargy;
- Scaling on the skin;
- Skin infections that reoccur;
- Infertility; and
- Intolerance to cold.

Treatment

Hypothyroidism is usually treatment with hormone replacement, as well as exercise and a low-fat diet. In addition to medication, synthetic hormones may be recommended for your dog.

i) Ingrown Eyelashes

Also known as trichiasis, this is a condition where the eyelashes grow into the eye and not away from the eye. It is believed to be caused by an abnormal structure of the face and can be an inherent condition.

Symptoms

The symptoms of trichiasis can be mistaken for other eye problems. Proper diagnosis is necessary for proper treatment. Symptoms that you may see are:

- Abnormal twitching of the eye;
- Swelling in the eyes and eye area;
- Tears; and
- Change in color in the iris.

Treatment

Treatment is often through surgery to remove the ingrown eyelashes.

j) Reverse Sneezing

Also known as reverse sneeze syndrome, it mainly consists of a series of rapid, loud, and forced inhalations through the nostrils, lasting anywhere between ten seconds and two minutes.

Chapter Ten: Alaskan Klee Kai Health

Symptoms

Attacks can occur randomly on an unpredictable basis, and the dog will usually have his head extended forward and stand still during this episode, during which time he will appear to be completely normal before and after the attack.

There is no loss of consciousness nor will he collapse, although sometimes his appearance may seem upsetting. Many dogs have these attacks throughout their lifetimes. The exact cause of reverse sneezing has not yet been uncovered, but it has been thought to have an association with sinusitis and other upper respiratory disorders.

It is believed that this attack is a conscious act by dogs to remove mucus from the nasal passages. To corroborate this theory, many dogs swallow at the end of the attack.

Treatment

This condition is usually not serious, but if it appears suddenly in an older dog or if episodes become more

Chapter Ten: Alaskan Klee Kai Health

severe or frequent, the nasal passages and throat should be examined immediately. If a nasal discharge is found or if a cough takes place, then you must notify your vet as soon as possible.

Treatment is not necessary when the episodes occur infrequently on a random basis.

Home treatments that have been reported to be successful include massaging the throat, blowing in the nose, and rapidly (and lightly) compressing the chest. Another effective treatment is to simply cover the dog's nose with your hands for 3 to 5 seconds and this will normally stop the reverse sneezing.

3. First Aid for your Alaskan Klee Kai

While I always recommend seeking the help of your veterinarian if your Alaskan Klee Kai is sick, I also recommend that owners know canine basic first aid. You can take several courses that will take you through more in-depth first aid but in this section, I will get you started.

a) First Aid Kit

Every home that has an Alaskan Klee Kai should have a first aid kit. The main reason is that the Alaskan Klee Kai is a curious breed and this means they can often get into peculiar situations. Having a first aid kit will not only reduce the chance of having to go to the vets but will also give your Klee Kai precious minutes in a life threatening situation.

To create a first aid kit, fill an easy to access Tupperware or water proof container with the following:

Chapter Ten: Alaskan Klee Kai Health

Important Telephone Numbers

Attach important telephone numbers to your container so you never have to search for the number during a crisis. Telephone numbers to have on hand are:

- Your Veterinarian's Office;
- Emergency Clinic: include the address to the clinic; and
- Poison Control Center.

Medicine

There are a number of medications that you can have on hand, which will help you manage a condition or treat it quickly. Always keep track of expiration dates on the medication in your first aid kit.

- Wound disinfectant for cuts;
- Sterile saline for washing out wounds;
- Antibiotic cream for cuts, and scrapes;
- Cortisone cream for itchy skin;
- Ear cleaning solution;
- Eye wash solution;
- Antibiotic eye ointment;
- Hydrogen peroxide for vomiting (only use at the discretion of your vet);
- Activated charcoal (only use at the discretion of your vet);
- Gas X or any gas medication to help prevent bloat;
- Anti-diarrhea medication; and

Chapter Ten: Alaskan Klee Kai Health

- Benadryl for allergies (only use at the discretion of your vet)

Equipment

While you may not feel you need a lot of equipment, I strongly recommend having most, if not all of the equipment listed. Sometimes, having the right equipment can mean your dog is treated at home and not at the vet's.

- Magnifying glass;
- Nail clippers;
- Cotton balls;
- Cotton swabs;
- Cold packs;
- Heat packs;
- Thermometer;
- Towels and blankets in case of emergency transport;
- Scissors;
- Penlight;
- Styptic powder to stop bleeding;
- Metal nail file;
- Oral syringe;
- Hemostat;
- KY Jelly;
- Eye dropper;
- Tweezers;

Chapter Ten: Alaskan Klee Kai Health

- Disposable gloves; and
- Bitter Apple.

In addition to these items, you should have a crate or pet carrier near your first aid kit for transporting your Alaskan Klee Kai.

Bandages and Other

Finally, you will want to make sure that you have bandages and a few odds and ends in your first aid kit. Things you should have are:

- Karo Syrup;
- Vitacal or other nutritional supplement;
- Gatorade for rehydration;
- Band-Aids;
- Square Gauze;
- Non-stick pads;
- First aid tape;
- Bandage rolls; and

Chapter Ten: Alaskan Klee Kai Health

- Vetwrap,

Once you have all your supplies, place the kit in an easy to access area.

b) Dealing with an Emergency

Now that you have your first aid kit all ready for your Alaskan Klee Kai, you are prepared for many of the little mishaps that life with a dog can bring. But are you ready for an emergency? Hopefully, the answer is "yes" but in this section, I will go over specific first aid that you should know.

Before I do I want to offer a few tips around dealing with an emergency.

Tip Number 1: Be Calm and Cautious

Although the first reaction is to panic, remain calm so your dog can feel that coming from you. In addition, always be cautious with handling the dog. If your Alaskan Klee Kai is hurt or frightened, moving too roughly can injure him further or frighten him more.

Tip Number 2: Only Move Your Dog if Necessary

Make sure that you only move your dog if he needs to be moved. Sometimes, lifting a dog too soon can compound the injury. If you can, wrap him carefully in a blanket and then move him.

Tip Number 3: Use your Voice

Alaskan Klee Kai often have a very strong bond with their owners and will react to your voice. If you talk to the dog in a loving and gentle manner, the dog will pick up on your

Chapter Ten: Alaskan Klee Kai Health

tone and relax. This will make first aid, or seeking medical help easier.

Tip Number 4: Keep your Alaskan Klee Kai Warm

Wrap your dog in a warm towel or apply a warm compress if it is unconscious or showing any signs of shock. Signs of early shock can include a rapid heart rate, panting, low temperature, bounding pulses, and a bright red color to the mucous membranes of the lips, gums, and tongue. By keeping your dog warm, you are less likely to complicate his condition.

Tip Number 5: Staunch Blood Loss

In the event of an injury with blood loss, make a compression bandage or manually compress the area to prevent as much blood loss as possible.

Remember that what you do in those first few minutes after a serious accident or emergency can, in some cases, mean the difference between life and death.

i) First Aid for Eye Injuries

When your Alaskan Klee Kai has an eye injury, it is important to look at the type of injury. If there is something in the eye, carefully flush the eye with an eye wash. You may need to have someone hold your dog's head while you spray the liquid over the eye.

If the dog has injured his eye and it is bleeding, take an eye dropper and carefully rinse the eyeball. You do not want to flush but simply moisten it. Once it is moistened, apply a compress gently over the eye. This will help staunch the bleeding and will keep the eye free from exposure.

Chapter Ten: Alaskan Klee Kai Health

Seek immediate veterinarian care after you have administered the first aid.

ii) First Aid for Seizures

Although not commonly seen in Alaskan Klee Kai, if your dog does have a seizure, you should contact your veterinarian as soon as possible. There can be several reasons for a seizure.

During the seizure, do not hold your dog. A dog in the middle of a seizure can be very scared and may bite.

In addition to staying clear, remove any objects that he could be hurt on. Finally, turn off any type of stimulation. Lights should be turned off, radios as well, people should try to stay quiet.

While the seizure is happening, time it and write down when it started and when it ended. This is important in case there are reoccurring seizures.

After the seizure has stopped, comfort your dog. Wrap him in a warm blanket and then sit with him until he begins to act normal. Follow the directions of your vet and take him in for an examination.

iii) First Aid for Heat Stroke

With their thick coats, it is possible for Alaskan Klee Kai to develop heat stroke or heat exhaustion. To help prevent heat stroke, do not leave your Klee Kai outside during hot weather. In addition – and especially, **NEVER LEAVE A DOG IN A HOT CAR.**

If your Alaskan Klee Kai does develop heat stroke, it is important to follow these steps:

Chapter Ten: Alaskan Klee Kai Health

1. Move the dog out of the hot area. Bring him to shade or inside.

2. Soak a towel with cold water.

3. Place the towel over the neck and head of your dog. Do not cover his eyes and keep his face clear of the fabric.

4. Repeat the process, wetting the towel down with cold water every few minutes.

5. If you cannot get to a vet, pour water over the dog's hind legs and abdomen.

6. While you are pouring water, massage the legs and then push the water off of the dog. Keeping the water moving will help cool the dog more.

As soon as you are able, take the dog to the veterinarian. Heat exhaustion should never be treated without the help of a trained professional.

iv) First Aid for Fractures

This is another emergency that will require veterinarian care. A fracture cannot be treated by an untrained person. While some people will try to create a splint, that can cause more harm than good so I strongly recommend against it.

Instead, take the time to muzzle your dog to keep him from biting. Then make a sling from a towel and blanket and keep him secure. Do not press on his chest or touch the area where the fracture is.

Place a blanket over him to keep your dog warm, especially if he is going into shock.

Chapter Ten: Alaskan Klee Kai Health

Take your pet to the veterinarian's office immediately.

v) First Aid for Burns

In the event of a burn, as long as it is not a severe burn that covers a large portion of the dog's body, you can treat the burn at home. If it is severe or covers a large area, seek medical attention immediately.

For small burns, flush the burn area with large quantities of water until the burn starts to cool. You can use a burn relief ointment but make sure that it is not toxic if ingested.

vi) First Aid for Choking

Choking can be a very scary situation for dog owners and it can happen very quickly. If your dog is choking, be sure to act quickly but be mindful that a choking dog is more likely to bite.

When the dog is choking, carefully grab his muzzle. Open his mouth and look inside it. If you can see the object that is causing him to choke, take a pair of tweezers and carefully pull the object out.

It is very important to be careful when you are doing this as it is easy to push the object further back into the throat. If you are unable to get the object out, seek medical help immediately.

If the dog stops breathing or collapses, place your Alaskan Klee Kai on his side. Place your hand over the rib cage and firmly strike the rib cage three to four times with the flat of your palm. Repeat as necessary on your journey to the vet.

Chapter Ten: Alaskan Klee Kai Health

While this may have no effect, administering this technique could force the air out of the lungs and force the obstruction out of your dog's throat.

vii) First Aid for Shock

This is another emergency that needs medical help and shock should be managed as you take your dog to the vets.

Wrap your dog in a warm blanket and keep him warm. Also, lie him down and try to keep his head level with the rest of his body. Stay calm and comfort your dog to help minimize his discomfort.

viii) First Aid for Bleeding

If your Alaskan Klee Kai has an injury that has resulted in bleeding, it is important to staunch the flow of blood. Using a thick gauze pad, apply pressure to the wound. The pressure will aid in stimulating the clotting mechanism of blood. If it is a minor injury, the bleeding will usually stop in a few minutes and you can then start cleaning the wound.

If it is severe, keep the pressure on the dog's wound. Wrap him in a blanket or use a heat pad to keep him warm. This will help prevent shock as you take him to the veterinarian for treatment.

ix) First Aid for Poisoning

Finally, if your dog is exposed to poison, it is important to immediately call poison control and/or your vet. They will guide you through the steps to take depending on the poison he has ingested. In the case of some toxins, you may be advised to administer active charcoal. In other

Chapter Ten: Alaskan Klee Kai Health

cases, hydrogen peroxide may be recommended to induce vomiting.

If the poison is on the skin or in the eyes, follow the directions on the container with the poison. Wash the area or flush it with water.

c) Cardiopulmonary resuscitation (CPR)

The final part of canine first aid that I want to touch on CPR. CPR should only be used in the event that your dog is not breathing. If he is breathing, do not administer CPR or you could cause more harm than good.

To administer CPR, follow these steps:

1. Remain calm.

2. Get someone to call your veterinarian.

3. Check the condition of your Alaskan Klee Kai. Is he unconscious?

4. Open your Klee Kai's mouth and pull out his tongue until it is lying flat. Check to see if there is an obstruction. If there is, see the section on choking.

5. If there isn't, close your Alaskan Klee Kai's mouth and hold it closed. Place your mouth on his nose and breathe outward.

6. Watch the chest and breathe inward until it expands.

7. Pause and count to 5, then repeat with a breath.

Chapter Ten: Alaskan Klee Kai Health

8. Check your dog's heartbeat. The best place to do this is right above the pad on his front paw.

9. Lay him on his right side.

10. Slip your one hand under his right side in the lower half of his chest.

11. Place your hand, palm down over the lower half of his left side. This is where the heart is on a dog.

12. Press down about half an inch into the chest. (The depth varies with a half inch for small dogs and an inch for medium-sized dogs.)

13. Press down repeatedly, about 100 to 150 times per minute for small dogs, 80 to 120 times per minute for larger animals.

14. If you are using rescue breathing, have someone help you. One person can press the chest for 4 to 5 seconds for every single breath.

15. Repeat until you can feel a heartbeat or do it while someone else is driving you and your Alaskan Klee Kai to the vet.

Although the information in this chapter will help you and your Alaskan Klee Kai, please remember that it should never replace the advice and care of a veterinarian.

Chapter Eleven: Breeding your Alaskan Klee Kai

Chapter 11: Breeding your Alaskan Klee Kai

Chapter Eleven: Breeding your Alaskan Klee Kai

Breeding your Alaskan Klee Kai is an important decision that every dog owner should make before they purchase a puppy. While we often think of breeding after the purchase, by choosing to breed beforehand, you can ensure that you are starting with the very best.

Remember to read the chapter on choosing a puppy in this book but one thing that I often stress is to find a mentor when you start breeding. While I have tried to be concise and fill this chapter with as much information as possible, breeding Alaskan Klee Kai is a constant learning experience and I cannot cover every challenge you may face.

What I can cover are tips on choosing the right dogs for your breeding program, how and when to breed, the simple facts about birthing a puppy and the schedule for raising puppies.

Chapter Eleven: Breeding your Alaskan Klee Kai

1. Choosing your Breeding Alaskan Klee Kai

The very first thing that you should do before deciding to breed your Alaskan Klee Kai is to choose the right dogs. While every dog can be bred, not every dog should be bred. It is important to really understand the breed standard of the Alaskan Klee Kai before you breed.

In general, when you are choosing a breeding pair, you want to look at the following.

Health

The pair of dogs should be healthy and in good condition. They should be in proportionate weight for their build and also pass a health test from your vet. They should be free of disease so there is no risk of that disease passing to the young.

If the vet voices any concerns over the health of your dogs, wait to breed them until they are in better health or choose different dogs.

Clearances

Clearances are very important to ensure the health of your puppies and the lifelong health of any dog you produce. As you know, Alaskan Klee Kai have several hereditary diseases so the health clearances you should get on your dogs are:

- Eyes Certified for Juvenile Cataracts;
- Factor VII Status;
- OFA Thyroid;
- OFA Cardiac; and

Chapter Eleven: Breeding your Alaskan Klee Kai

- OFA Knees.

In addition to these clearances, you should have the dogs tested for brucellosis, which is a canine sexually transmitted disease (STD). Any dog that is being bred should be clear. Brucellosis can cause sterility in both males and females and can cause the dam to abort the puppies.

Registration

At one time, the Alaskan Klee Kai was not a registered dog. Today, the breed is established and has been accepted by the UKC. Breeding UKC-registered dogs will help ensure that the dogs produced are purebred. Another registry that you can use with the Alaskan Klee Kai is the American Kennel Club (AKC) registry.

Temperament

Temperament is as important as health when it comes to breeding. Studies have proven that temperament is a hereditary trait so it is important to breed dogs with a sound temperament. If you have a dog with aggression or skittishness, it is recommended that you do not breed the dog.

Blood Lines

Another factor that you want to take into account is the blood line. Is it a strong pedigree? Do the two pedigrees share a lot of relations? While line breeding does occur, I do not recommend it for people new to breeding. There are a lot of factors with line breeding and can lead to health problems if it is not done properly.

Chapter Eleven: Breeding your Alaskan Klee Kai

Age

Something that is very important with breeding is the age of the dogs. Females should be no younger than 18 months of age for breeding and males should not be younger than 15 months of age.

If you are getting clearances, some clearances cannot be done before the dog is 24 months of age so it is important to wait at least until that stage.

On the other end of the age spectrum, you should not breed a bitch after she is 7 years of age. Males can be bred for many years after that, however, the quality and quantity of sperm is affected by age.

Physical Traits

Finally, you will want to choose a pair according to the physical traits of both dogs. While they both should be good examples of the breed, you should look at what each dog can bring to the puppies.

For instance, if both dogs have excellent ears according to the breed standard, the odds are very high that the puppies

Chapter Eleven: Breeding your Alaskan Klee Kai

will inherit those ears. A good coat on a female may be passed on to the puppies, even if the male has a coat that is not as desirable. A good body shape on the male may be passed on to the puppies and so on.

Choosing complementary traits will only improve your puppies and your lines.

While many people promote showing, it is not a prerequisite for breeding. It is something I recommend doing with your dogs, along with obedience training. However, showing is elective.

Before you do make that final decision on what to breed, it is important to remember that breeding is a responsibility. There is often very little money to be earned when doing it properly and it is a full-time commitment.

While the dam will help with the care, the puppies will take a lot of your care as well during those first 8 weeks. In addition, breeders should be prepared to re-home any of their puppies if they are returned for some reason.

Breeding is not for the faint of heart by any means but one thing is for sure, cuddling a newborn Alaskan Klee Kai in your arms is worth all the work, money, and commitment.

2. Breeding your Alaskan Klee Kai

Now that you have your breeding pair, it is time to get down to business and breed your dog. While it may seem like a simple thing, breeding an Alaskan Klee Kai can be challenging. The dogs will instinctually mate, but a successful litter requires a lot of knowledge.

Chapter Eleven: Breeding your Alaskan Klee Kai

a) The Heat

When a female dog reaches sexual maturity, she will begin what is known as a heat. A heat or heat cycle is when the female will begin bleeding and is ready to be bred. For Alaskan Klee Kai, the first heat is usually around six months of age; however, a dog should never be bred on her first heat or before the age of 18 months to 2 years.

With heat cycles, some females will take longer to have their first heat and it is not uncommon for an Alaskan Klee Kai to be closer to a year of age or even up to 2 years when she has her first heat. After the first heat, you can expect the dog to go into heat every six to eight months. Some females will have a heat more frequently and others less frequently.

Symptoms of the heat begin before the discharge. Often the vulva begins to swell and the female will begin licking her back end and vulva more. In addition, she may urinate

Chapter Eleven: Breeding your Alaskan Klee Kai

more frequently and if you have any male dogs in the home, you may notice them paying more attention to her than normally.

The female will begin to have a bloody discharge and this can vary in heaviness between females and even heats. Some females have very little discharge and other females have a lot.

The heat cycle lasts about 3 weeks but it is important to not let the female near a male until about 4 weeks after the start of her heat. If you are planning on breeding her, breeding will take place about 9 to 11 days after her heat starts.

b) Natural or Artificial?

When you are breeding, you can choose between allowing the dogs to breed naturally and artificial insemination (AI). Many breeders learn how to do AIs themselves however, in the event of frozen sperm, you would need to have the AI done by a veterinarian, specifically a reproductive veterinarian.

Natural breeding is when you allow the male dog to mount the female and tie. This is often the more preferred way to breed.

With AI, the sperm is delivered to the vagina through a sterilized, medical device. There are several reasons why you would use AI and these are:

- Stud dog is too far away;
- A dominant female who will not allow a male to mount;
- An inexperienced stud dog;

Chapter Eleven: Breeding your Alaskan Klee Kai

- A persistent hymen in a bitch; and
- Size incompatibility.

AI is less likely to spread an STD but it usually leads to smaller litter sizes. Also, it is important to properly judge when ovulation occurs, which can be difficult and is usually done with progesterone testing by your vet.

If you are able to breed naturally, then I recommend that you breed your dogs with a natural tie (dog mating position in which both dogs are virtually locked together). If you are not in a position to do that, then use AI.

c) When to Breed

You have the stud dog, a bitch in heat and you have made the decision to go with a natural tie. Terrific, you are ready to start breeding soon...but maybe not right away.

Breeding times differs between female to female, although the general rule of thumb is between days 9 and 11. If you have the male in the home, you can begin breeding as soon as the female starts accepting him.

The rule of thumb is to breed every other day. This gives the sperm time to recover in numbers and the male will have better sperm numbers.

If you do not have a male, you can do progesterone testing to try to narrow down when your female is most fertile. Progesterone testing is done with a blood test. .A vaginal smear can also be ordered, although this is not as accurate.

When using progesterone testing, follow the guidelines of your veterinarian.

Chapter Eleven: Breeding your Alaskan Klee Kai

Although testing the dog is an excellent way to identify if your female dog is ready to be bred, you can also see this with her behavior. A female that is ready to be bred will exhibit the following:

- Vaginal discharge will turn to a light pink or straw color.
- The female will back up into the male.
- She will hold her tail to the side, this is known as flagging.
- She will be playful with the male.
- She will stand still when the male is sniffing her.
- She won't attack the male when he tries to mount her.

When you see these signs, your female is ready to be bred.

Chapter Eleven: Breeding your Alaskan Klee Kai

d) The Act of Breeding

When your female is ready to be bred, it is time to let the dogs do their job. During this time, you should allow the stud dog and the bitch to be together. Never leave them unattended as injuries can occur if the female attacks the male or she becomes scared.

The stud dog will spend some time sniffing the backend of the female and he may begin to lick the vulva. The female will stand still and will move her tail out of the way. She will also back into the male.

As he builds excitement, the male will mount the female, wrapping his front legs around the hips of the female. He will begin to thrust against the female and his penis will enter the vulva.

During this action, the glans penis will come out of the sheath, which is a bright red organ. The penis will extend into the vulva until the dog locks with the female. Once the lock happens, the male and female cannot be separated. Do not try to separate them as you can hurt both the male and the female.

Once they are locked, the male will lift his leg over the backend of the female and then turn so they are standing with their back ends together. The penis will bend but will still be inserted in the vulva.

Dogs will remain locked for 10 to 30 minutes until the penis loses enough of its swelling to release from the lock.

One myth that abounds is that a female cannot get pregnant if there is no tie. This is not true. When the dog is thrusting, sperm is released. The fluid that is released when they are

Chapter Eleven: Breeding your Alaskan Klee Kai

locked is very low in sperm and is used to push the sperm through the cervix.

Allow your dogs to mate only once per day and then wait a day before you breed again.

e) Is She Pregnant?

The gestational period for dogs is between the 63 to 65 days after the time of first breeding, but you can have some additional or fewer days depending on the individual dog.

One of the biggest hurdles that breeders go through is whether a dog is pregnant. This is very difficult to determine because a female dog goes through the same hormone changes whether she is pregnant or not. In fact, even a female who has not been bred can present the symptoms of pregnancy.

During the first month, you will notice very few symptoms. The female may have morning sickness where her appetite decreases, though some females are not affected at all.

After the first 30 days, the dog will begin to show some symptoms. Symptoms of pregnancy are:

- Nipple growth;
- Pinking of the nipples;
- Decreased appetite early on;
- Increased appetite around week 6;
- Clinginess and other behavior changes;
- Pear shape of the abdomen; and
- Weight gain.

Chapter Eleven: Breeding your Alaskan Klee Kai

At 30 to 35 days, you can have an ultrasound done to confirm pregnancy. Numbers are not usually given during ultrasounds as it is very difficult to count the puppies. After 45 days of gestation, an x-ray can be done and the puppies can be counted at that time. It is important to note that sometimes counts are wrong since puppies will hide in the x-ray.

3. Birthing your Pups

So your female is pregnant and the time is drawing closer to when she will be whelping her puppies. This is an exciting time but it is also a busy time for you. It is very important to have all your supplies ready and to begin preparing for the puppies a few weeks before their arrival.

a) Whelping Supplies

The whelping supplies are essential for helping your Alaskan Klee Kai whelp her puppies. In the best case scenario, you will need to interact very little with the labor. In the worst case, you could be looking at having to rush

Chapter Eleven: Breeding your Alaskan Klee Kai

your pregnant mom to the vet clinic for an emergency C-section.

In addition, even an easy whelping can result in puppies in distress so it is important to have the tools on hand to help the puppies.

Things you will need in your whelping supplies are:

- *Whelping box:* This should be a square box that the mother can deliver and raise her puppies in. You can make the box yourself or you can purchase premade whelping boxes.

- *Blankets:* Have a lot of blankets and towels on hand for your whelping box. Labor is messy and that means you have to exchange the bedding in the whelping box several times during labor.

- *Newspaper:* In addition to blankets, have a large amount of newspaper to put down during the whelping process. Again, you are going to be going through a lot of it.

- *Basket:* A laundry basket or Tupperware container to put the puppies into when the female is birthing another puppy.

- *Hot water bottles:* Water bottles are needed for the basket so puppies can stay warm when they are not with their mother. Puppies will cuddle up to the water bottles if they are cold and will move away if they are too warm.

- *Scale:* Have a kitchen scale so you can properly weigh each puppy as it is born. This will be a tool you use throughout the time the litter is with you

Chapter Eleven: Breeding your Alaskan Klee Kai

since you will want to weigh the puppies on a regular basis.

- ***Notebook and Pens:*** Create a notebook that charts the progress of each individual puppy. Start with the puppy's sex, identifier, date of birth, presentation at birth, time born, coloration and weight. This will help you keep track of each puppy.

- ***Identifier:*** This can be yarn, puppy collars, or nail polish. Basically, it is anything that you can use to identify each puppy. Use the yarn like a collar on each puppy so you can identify each individual puppy right from birth. Use the same collar color for that puppy throughout the 8 weeks that you have the puppies.

In addition to those items, have the following items available in a kit and be sure to sterilize all of the instruments such as the scissors and hemostats:

- Sharp scissors;
- Hemostats;
- Surgical gloves;
- Iodine swabs;
- Alcohol swabs;
- Lubricating jelly such as K-Y;
- Digital thermometer;
- Vaseline;
- Nursing bottles for puppies;
- Liquid puppy vitamins;

Chapter Eleven: Breeding your Alaskan Klee Kai

- Puppy formula;
- Energizing glucose drops; and
- Bulb syringe.

Place all of the items into an easy to access container and have it close to your whelping box.

b) Before Labor

As you know, the gestation period for dogs is about 63 to 65 days, give or take a few days. It is important to monitor your dog during the days leading up to the delivery. Around day 56 to 58, the female should start searching for a nesting site. Encourage her to nest in the whelping box by sitting by it and calmly petting her. Don't discourage her scratching at the bedding as this is normal.

In addition to this, you should start taking her temperature about a week before her due date. The average temperature of your female will be between 99 to 101°F (37.22 to 38.33°C). Mark down her temperature each day and closer to the due date, start checking her temperature several times per day.

The reason why we are watching the temperatures is because we are waiting for a temperature spike and then drop. About 48 hours before labor, her temperature will have spike up to about 101.5°F (38.6°C) or higher. Within 24 hours after that, the temperature will drop. Once it gets to below 98°F (36.7°C), you will have 12 to 24 hours before the litter is expected.

c) First Stage Labor

When she has her final temp drop, you will start to notice a number of symptoms that your female is going into labor. For about 2 to 12 hours, your female will become restless.

Chapter Eleven: Breeding your Alaskan Klee Kai

She may start to nest even more than she did before, or she may become very stressed wanting to wander around the house.

You may see some shivering and she will probably change positions frequently. Her eyes will dilate and she will watch you and want to be with you. Try to stay near the whelping box so she can settle in.

She may lose her appetite during this time and it is not uncommon for your Alaskan Klee Kai female to vomit. Also, she may try to go to the bathroom and not be able to. This is caused by the pressure building up in her belly.

If you take your Alaskan Klee Kai outside to go to the bathroom, keep her on a leash and check the spot where she squatted. It is not uncommon for puppies to be born outside.

Finally, you may see some mucus being discharged from the vulva.

Chapter Eleven: Breeding your Alaskan Klee Kai

d) Second Stage of Labor

During the second stage of labor, your female should start digging at her bedding even more. You will also notice your Alaskan Klee Kai looking at her back end more frequently and she may start licking her vulva.

Shivering is more noticeable and she will have periods where she is panting heavily. You may be able to see mild contractions going across her belly or you may feel a tightening of her stomach.

Again, your Alaskan Klee Kai may vomit and she may ask to go outside more frequently. Remember to stay with her when she goes to the bathroom to make sure a pup isn't born outside.

At this time, if the discharge turns to a dark green color, seek medical help. Dark green discharge is normal but only after a puppy is born. If it is before, it can indicate a life threatening problem for both your bitch and your litter.

e) Third Stage of Labor

It is the stage of labor when the puppies begin to be birthed. During this time, the contractions will become stronger and you will be able to see them. They will also occur closer together.

The Alaskan Klee Kai female may vomit during this time and you will notice that she will begin pushing and grunting. Some females will squat when they have their puppies, others will lie on their side so let the female decide how she is going to birth the puppy.

As she is pushing, you will see a membrane sac filled with water and the puppy come out of the vulva. Puppies are

Chapter Eleven: Breeding your Alaskan Klee Kai

born in their own sac and it may burst while being delivered or as the female breaks it.

Puppies may be born both front paws first or breeched in which their tail or back paws present first. The puppy is followed by the afterbirth. Although it is unclear what benefits a female will get from eating the placenta and membranes, it is a natural instinct for females to do so. It has been linked to better milk production so I allow females to eat the membranes and afterbirth. I take a note of each afterbirth I see. It can be dangerous if the female retains an afterbirth. Retained placentas can lead to uterine infections and toxicity. If you suspect a retained placenta, immediately contact your veterinarian.

Puppies are usually born in quick succession of two or three puppies, and then you will have a wait of about an hour or so before additional puppies are born.

The process of birthing can last up to 24 hours, depending on the size of the litter.

Chapter Eleven: Breeding your Alaskan Klee Kai

If you find that the female is pushing for longer than 30 minutes without seeing a puppy, contact your veterinarian and follow his advice. It could mean that a puppy is stuck in the birth canal.

Also, if there is a long period of time between puppies, contact your veterinarian, especially if you are expecting more puppies.

When the puppies are born, allow them to nurse from their mother between contractions. Every time she is ready to push, remove the puppies to their basket. This keeps the mother from being distracted by the puppies and she is less likely to sit on the puppy or hurt it.

Try to let her do the work herself. If you get too involved, you could cause her to stop laboring. Only get involved if she looks like she needs help.

In between puppies, weigh the puppy that was most recently born, jot down all the notes on the puppy and place an identifier collar on the puppy.

Watching a litter being born is a very exciting thing but make sure you are prepared for any problems. Also, keep the whelping room quiet and calm.

Chapter Eleven: Breeding your Alaskan Klee Kai

It is also important to note that in the weeks after giving birth, the gland that is responsible for regulating the parathyroid hormone, which in turn regulates the amount of calcium which is stored within the mother, can become depleted.

When the bitch's milk starts to come in, and the demand for calcium is suddenly increased, the parathyroid gland is unable to respond quickly enough for her needs to be fully met. This can lead to her body contracting convulsively, which will effectively limit her movement. This condition is known as eclampsia.

Once diagnosed with eclampsia, the new mother will be prescribed calcium supplementation. Alternatively, foods such as cottage cheese, goat's milk, or mature cheddar will also help in supporting her to heal through this phase.

4. Raising Pups

Raising pups is a fun activity and for the first few weeks, the mother does the majority of the work. She will clean the puppies and feed them. However, it does not mean that you have nothing to do—you will be very busy with your own chores. Below is a chart of what you need to do with the puppies while they are growing.

Age	Puppy Development	Chores List
Week 1	The puppies sleep the majority of the time. When they are awake, they will crawl and squirm towards warmth and milk. The puppies will have their eyes and	• Chart Weight twice a day • Trim nails at the end of the week. • Handle the

Chapter Eleven: Breeding your Alaskan Klee Kai

	ears closed and are very helpless at this age.	puppies daily to check their health and start neurological stimulation • Clean the bedding daily. • Monitor the mom and her health. • Keep whelping box at about 85°F (29.4°C)
Week 2	Puppies are beginning to move around more and they are awake for longer periods. Eyes will begin to open at day 8 to 10, ears will open near the end of week 2 or beginning of week 3.	• Trim nails at the end of the week. • Hold the puppies in different positions. • Monitor the mother and her health. • Clean bedding daily. • Weigh puppies once a day.
Week 3	Eyes and ears will be open by the end of this week and they will become more active. They will start trying to walk	• Continue to handle the puppies. • Trim nails at

Chapter Eleven: Breeding your Alaskan Klee Kai

	and will be able to go to the bathroom without stimulation from mother. They will begin to play and their little teeth are erupting.	end of the week. • Begin socializing the puppy to things such as grooming items. • Weigh puppies every other day. • Monitor the mother and her health. • Clean bedding daily
Week 4	During this week, the puppies will be more playful and will begin growling. They will also be eating food and while they may nurse occasionally, mom will have less to do with them but should still be with them a lot. Cleaning up poop will be your job as soon as they start eating things other than their mother's milk.	• Continue to handle the puppies. • Trim nails at end of the week. • Begin socializing the puppy to other things such as noises and other animals in your home. • Begin weaning process. Start with milk replacer once a day for two

Chapter Eleven: Breeding your Alaskan Klee Kai

		days. Then add a mushy food once per day. • Weigh puppies every other day. • Monitor the mother and her health. • Clean bedding daily
Week 5	Puppies are more alert and they will be active. You will start to notice pack order and may even see sexual play. Puppies will grow quickly during this time.	• Shift the food to an oatmeal-like consistency, add one extra meal a day. • Weigh puppies two to three times each week. • Reduce the mother's diet to stop her milk production. • Start reducing the amount of liquid in the puppies' food. • Continue to handle the puppies.

Chapter Eleven: Breeding your Alaskan Klee Kai

		• Trim nails at end of the week. • Continue socializing the puppies to a range of stimuli. • Clean bedding daily.
Week 6	Puppies are developing quickly and they are developing their own personalities. Mom will be with the puppies less at this stage.	• Give each puppy alone time. • Weigh the puppies weekly. • Continue reducing the amount of liquid in the puppies' food. • Continue to handle the puppies. • Trim nails at end of the week. • Continue socializing the puppies to a range of stimuli. • Clean bedding daily.

Chapter Eleven: Breeding your Alaskan Klee Kai

Week 7	Puppies will be able to hear and see fully at this stage. They will be very inquisitive and can get into some problems.	<ul><li>Give each puppy alone time.</li><li>Weigh the puppies weekly.</li><li>Puppies should be fully weaned and on puppy food.</li><li>Continue to handle the puppies.</li><li>Trim nails at end of the week.</li><li>Continue socializing the puppies to a range of stimuli.</li><li>Clean bedding daily.</li></ul>
Week 8	Puppies are at the age where they can start going to their new homes. This is the week when a fear period can occur so make sure you do not stress them too much.	<ul><li>Give each puppy alone time.</li><li>Weigh the puppies weekly.</li><li>Trim nails at end of the week.</li><li>Continue</li></ul>

Chapter Eleven: Breeding your Alaskan Klee Kai

		socializing the puppies to a range of stimuli.
		• Clean bedding daily.
		• Start training puppies that have not left for their new home.

Raising a litter of puppies is a lot of work so before you breed your dog, I strongly recommend that you do a lot of research and be ready for the commitment.

Chapter Twelve: Common Terms

Chapter 12: Common Terms

Chapter Twelve: Common Terms

So you are interested in dogs and the Alaskan Klee Kai? While most of the vocabulary dealing with dogs is the same as with any other animal, there are a few terms that you should be aware of.

In this chapter, I will go over common terms that you may encounter as you enjoy life with your Alaskan Klee Kai.

Agility: The Alaskan Klee Kai thoroughly enjoys the sport of dog agility. This is a sport in which the dog handler guides and instructs the dog through a course of obstacles while being timed. Accuracy through this obstacle course is paramount. The dogs must complete the obstacle course without a leash or toys (or food) as incentives. The handler can only use voice, movement and various body signals in order to direct the dog.

Acquired Immunity: When a dog has developed antibodies that enables it to resist a disease. Acquired Immunity is often seen in newborn puppies as they get antibodies from their dam. It is also seen after vaccinations.

Chapter Twelve: Common Terms

Acute Disease: Refers to a disease or illness that manifests quickly.

Adoption: To take an animal or person in as your own. Is commonly used to describe bringing in a dog from a shelter or rescue but can also be used when purchasing a puppy.

Afterbirth: A term used to describe the fetal membranes and placenta that is expelled after the birth of a puppy.

Agent: A person who trains, works or shows a dog. Also known as a handler.

Agility: A dog sport where the dogs will navigate through obstacles during a timed event. Alaskan Klee Kai do very well in agility sports.

Albino: A genetic condition where an animal is born with white hair and pink eyes.

Allergen: A particle that triggers an allergic reaction. Found in dog hair or more specifically in a protein that is found in dog dander.

Almond eyes: Eyes that have an elongated shape.

Alpha: The top dog in a social pack, usually the most dominant dog. Also refers to a form of training.

Alter: A term used to describe neutering or spaying.

Amble: Used to describe a gait where the dog's legs on either side move almost as a pair.

*Anal Glands: S*acks or glands that are found on either side of the anus. All dogs use the substance secreted by the gland to mark territory.

Chapter Twelve: Common Terms

Anestrous: The period of time between heats in female dogs.

Ankle: Found in the hind legs, it is the area between the second thigh and metatarsus where there is a collection of bones. Also known as the hock.

Anterior: The front of the dog.

Apron: Refers to longer hair on the chest, also known as the frill.

Arm: Refers to the area between the shoulder and elbow of the dog's front legs.

Articulation: Refers to the area where bones meet.

Artificial Insemination: Used during breeding, it refers to using artificial means to place semen into the bitch's reproductive tract.

Asymptomatic: When a dog has a disease but is not exhibiting symptoms.

Awn hairs: Seen on dogs with double coats, it is the section of undercoat that is long and has a coarse texture to it. It should be slightly longer than the downy undercoat but shorter than the outer coat.

Back: The area on the dog that extends from the shoulders to the rump of the dog.

Back crossing: Refers to the act of breeding a dog to its parent.

Backyard Breeder: Refers to a breeder who breeds dogs for profit with little care for the health of the dogs and puppies.

Chapter Twelve: Common Terms

Bad Mouth: When a dog has crooked teeth.

Balance: Used to describe the symmetry of the dog as well as its proportion.

Bandy Legs: Refers to legs that bend outward.

Barrel: Refers to the area around the ribs of a dog.

Barrel Hocks: Refers to legs where the hock turns outward, which makes the paws turn inward. Also known as spread hocks.

Beefy: When a dog has too much weight in his hindquarters.

Behavior Modification: Using training and conditioning to control, alter or teach specific behaviors.

Bitch: The common term used to describe a female dog.

Chapter Twelve: Common Terms

Bite: When a dog places his teeth on something. Also used to describe the position of the upper and lower teeth when the dog has his mouth closed.

Blocky: When the dog has a square like shape to his head.

Blooded: Refers to a dog with a pedigree that comes from good breeding.

Bloodline: The pedigree of the dog.

Blunt Muzzle: When a dog has a square shaped muzzle.

Board: When the dog is placed in a location where the care, feeding and housing of the dog is paid for. Usually used when owners are on vacation.

Body Length: Measured from the front of the breastbone to the pelvis to identify how long a dog is.

Booster Vaccination: Injections given to a dog to boost the immunity they have to specific diseases. Usually given on a yearly basis.

Bossy: When a dog has shoulder muscles that have been over developed.

Brace: Refers to two dogs that are presented as a pair. They should be of the same breed.

Break: When there is a change in coloration between the puppy and adult coats.

Breastbone: The area on the chest where 8 bones connect to form the area.

Chapter Twelve: Common Terms

Breech Birth: The presentation of the puppy at birth. In breech, the puppy comes out hind end first. Breech birth is very common in dogs.

Breeches: Fur on the upper thighs that is longer and fringe like. Also known as pants, culottes and trousers.

Breed: Refers to a group of dogs that share common characteristics, traits and gene pool.

Breed Club: Refers to a group of enthusiasts dedicated to a specific breed.

Breeder: Any person who produces a litter or breeds a dog.

Breed Rescue: A rescue group that specialized in finding homes for unwanted dogs of a specific breed.

Breed Standard: A description of a breed that describes the physical characteristics as well as temperament to expect in a set breed.

Breeding Particulars: The information about a breeding or litter such as the parents, sex and color of the puppy and the date of birth.

Brick Shaped: A dog that has a rectangular shape.

Brisket: Usually refers to the breastbone or sternum, however, it can also refer to the entire chest and thorax of the dog.

Brood Bitch: Used to refer to a female dog that has or will be used for breeding.

Brows: The ridge above the eye.

Brush: When a tail has a heavy amount of hair on it.

Chapter Twelve: Common Terms

Brushing: Refers to a gait where the dog's legs brush against each other when he walks.

Butterfly: Refers to a nose that has only a small or partial amount of pigmentation on it.

Buttocks: The rump of the dog.

By-products: Found in food labels, it refers to any food that is not suitable for human consumption.

Camel Back: A dog that has an arched back

Canid: Refers to any animal in the canidae family such as dogs, wolves and foxes.

Canine: A term for dog.

Canine Teeth: The largest teeth found in the dog's mouth. They are long, curved teeth on either side of the mouth, top and bottom. Also known as eye teeth.

Canter: A run where the dog has three beats.

Cape: Refers to longer hair over the shoulders.

Carnivore: An animal that eats only the flesh of other animals.

Carpals: The bones found in the wrist.

Carrier: When a dog carries a disease that it can transmit to other animals without showing any signs of the disease.

Castrate: When the dog's testicles are removed.

Cat Foot: Refers to a paw that is round with high-arched toes.

Chapter Twelve: Common Terms

Cheek: The area between the lips and front of ears just under the eyes.

Chest: The area around the ribs.

Chippendale Front: When the dog's forelegs push out at the elbows on the front legs and the paws turn out.

Chiseled: A dog with a head free of bumps and bulges.

Chronic Disease: Refers to a disease that will last indefinitely.

Cleft Palate: When the two halves of the mouth do not fuse properly. It is a birth defect.

Clipping: When a dog's back paw hits the front paw when walking.

Cloddy: A dog that is thick and heavy.

Close Mating: Used to describe the act of breeding the same female shortly after her previous litter was whelped. The period of time would be less than 4 months and 15 days.

Close Coupled: Refers to a short length of body between the last set of ribs and the hind quarters.

Coarse: A dog that is not refined. Also refers to the texture of the coat when it has a hard or rough texture.

Coat: The fur that covers the dog.

Cobby: A dog with a short body.

Colostrum: The clear to yellowish milk produced by a dam during the first few days after her puppies are born.

Chapter Twelve: Common Terms

Concaveation: When a spayed female produces milk.

Condition: The overall look and health of the dog.

Conformation: A term used to describe the physical and temperament traits of a breed. Alaskan Klee Kai have a breed standard that is approved by the UKC. All dogs should conform to this standard as closely as possible.

Congenital: A disease or condition that is present at birth.

Coupling: Refers to the part of the dog's body that is between the ribs and hind quarters.

Cow-hocked: When the dog's hocks turn inward and cause the feet to turn outward.

Crate: Also known as a kennel, the crate is a container that is used for housing dogs.

Crest: The area on the neck that is arched.

Crossbred: When a dog has a dam and sire from different breeds. Also known as a cur.

Croup: The area around the pelvic girdle.

Crown: The top of the head.

Culottes: Fur on the upper thighs that is longer and fringe like. Also known as pants, breeches and trousers.

Cur: When a dog has a dam and sire from different breeds. Also known as a crossbreed.

Cynology: The study of dogs and canines.

Chapter Twelve: Common Terms

Dam: A female dog that is pregnant or has puppies. Also refers to the female parent or mother.

Dander: The skin that is sloughed off of the dog.

Date of Whelping: Refers to the date when the puppies are born.

Dealer: An individual who buys puppies from a breeder and then sells the puppies to others. It is recommended that you avoid puppy dealers.

Deep Chest: A dog or dog breed that has a longer chest or rib cage.

Dentition: The number of teeth in an adult dog, which is 42.

Dewclaw: The claw that is found on the inside of the leg above the paw.

Digit: Refers to a toe.

Dock: The act of cutting a dog's tail short.

Dog: Refers to canines. It is also the term used for a male canine.

Domed Skull: A skull that is rounded.

Domesticated: A term used to describe any animal that has been tamed.

Dominance: When a dog has more assertive characteristics. Also describes when a single dog has more influence over other dogs, i.e. he is the dominant dog of the pack.

Chapter Twelve: Common Terms

Double coat: Refers to a type of dog coat that has two coats; the soft undercoat that provides warmth and the topcoat that provides protection from the weather and terrain.

Down Hairs: The shortest hairs on a dog, which are usually soft and downy in texture.

Dudley Nose: A nose that has no pigmentation.

Elbow: The area on the posterior of the forearm.

Elbows Out: When a dog's elbows turn away from the body.

Embryo: A term used to describe an undeveloped fetus.

Entire: A dog that has not been altered and its reproductive system is complete.

Estrus: The period of a dog's heat cycle when the female is most receptive to being mated. It precedes ovulation

Euthanasia: The practice of ending life through medical means.

Even Bite: When the lower and upper incisors have no overlap.

Expression: The features of the head and how they look.

F1: The offspring of a direct crossing of two purebred dogs.

F2: The offspring of one F1 parent and one purebred parent. Could also refer to the offspring of two F1 parents.

Chapter Twelve: Common Terms

F3: The offspring of one F1 parent and one F2 parent. Could also refer to the offspring of two F2 parents.

Fangs: The canine teeth.

Feathering: Long hair on the ears, tail, legs or body that has a fringe like appearance.

Feral: A dog that has returned to a wild state.

Fetus: The unborn puppy.

Fever: An indication that there is an illness. The body temperature rises to over 103°F in dogs.

Fiddle Front: When a dog's elbows and paws turn out but the pasterns are close together.

Fillers: Found in dog food, it is a chemical or low quality, difficult to digest food that adds weight to the dog food.

Fixed: A term to describe a dog that has been neutered or spayed.

Flank: The side of a dog's body that is between the hip and last rib.

Flat-Sided: A dog that has flat ribs, the desired shape is rounded.

Floating Rib: In dogs, the 13th rib is not attached to the other ribs.

Flying Trot: A run where all four of the dog's paws are off the ground for a second on each half stride.

Foster Mother: A female dog that is nursing puppies that are not her own.

Chapter Twelve: Common Terms

Fresh Extended Semen: This is used in breeding where semen is extracted from a male dog and an extender is placed in the semen to expand the lifespan of the semen.

Frill: Refers to longer hair on the chest, also known as the apron.

Front: The part of the dog's body that is in the front. This is the forelegs, shoulder line, chest, head, etc.

Frozen Semen: Used in breeding, it is semen that is extracted from the male dog and frozen to be used at a later date.

Furrow: An indentation found in the centre of the skull to the top of the dog's muzzle.

Gait: The pattern of steps when a dog is in movement.

Gallop: When the dog is running.

Gaskin: The lower thigh on the dog.

Genetically Linked Defects: Health problems that are passed from parent to offspring.

Gestation Period: A breeding term - it is the time period between mating and birth.

Get: The offspring of a dog.

Grooming: Brushing, bathing, trimming and caring for the hygienic needs of the dog's coat.

Guard Hair: The hair that is stiffer and longer than the normal hair of the dog. Usually protects the dog from the terrain and weather.

Chapter Twelve: Common Terms

Hackles: The hairs found on the back of a dog's neck. It will stand up when the dog is angry or frightened.

Handler: A person who trains, works or shows a dog, also known as an agent.

Haunch Bones: Term referring to the hip bones.

Haw: The third eyelid found in dogs.

Head: This is used to describe the front portion of the dog, which includes the muzzle, face, ears and cranium.

Heat: When a dog begins to produce a blood like discharge from her vulva to signal that she is ready to be bred.

Height: Height is always measured from the bottom of the paw (ground) to the tallest point on the withers (shoulders).

High in Rear: A dog that has a back end that is higher than its shoulders.

Hock: Found in the hind legs, it is the area between the second thigh and metatarsus where there is a collection of bones, also known as the ankle.

Housebreak: Training a puppy not to urinate or defecate in the house.

Immunization: When shots are given to a dog to help produce immunity to a specific disease.

Imported Semen: When frozen semen is imported from another country.

In and In: Refers to any form of inbreeding in dogs where little consideration is given to the results.

Chapter Twelve: Common Terms

Inbreeding: Mating two dogs that are closely related. These include mother to son, daughter to son, sibling to sibling.

Incisors: The upper and lower teeth found at the front of the mouth between the canines. Adult dogs have six upper and six lower.

Incubation Period: The period of time between being infected with a disease and the first symptom appearing.

Interbreeding: Breeding dogs that are of different breeds.

Jacobsen's Organ: This is an organ located in the dog's mouth, specifically on the roof, that functions as a sensory organ for taste and smell.

Keel: The rounded area of the chest.

Kennel: Also known as a crate, the kennel is a container that is used for housing dogs. Also used to describe a place that houses and/or breeds dogs.

Chapter Twelve: Common Terms

Knuckling Over: A condition seen primarily in puppies where the wrist joints flex forward when the dog is standing.

Lactation: Production of milk by the mammary glands of a female dog.

Lead: Synonym to a leash.

Leather: The part of the outer ear that is supported by cartilage.

Line: The pedigree or family of dogs who are related.

Line Breeding: When a dog is bred to another member of its blood line such as grandfather to granddaughter, aunt to nephew, uncle to niece.

Litter: The puppies that are produced during a whelping. It can refer to one puppy or several.

Litter Complement: Refers to the number of puppies of each sex in a litter.

Litter Registration: A record with a kennel club of a litter.

Lumbering: Refers to a dog with a gait that is awkward.

Mad Dog: Refers to a dog that has rabies

Marking: A behavior primarily of males, although it can be seen in females, where a dog will urinate to establish the boundaries of its territory.

Markings: Used to describe the patterns found on a dog's coat.

Mask: When there is dark shading on the face.

Chapter Twelve: Common Terms

Mate: When a male dog and female dog are bred.

Maternal Immunity: Seen in newborn puppies, it is a resistance to disease that is temporarily passed from mother to pup.

Measure Out: When a dog's height is larger than the breed standard.

Microchip: A small chip that is inserted under the skin. It contains a code that can be scanned and all the owner's information for the dog can be pulled up.

Milk Teeth: The puppy's first teeth, which will fall out to make way for adult teeth during the first year of life.

Molars: The square, posterior teeth that is used for chewing.

Mongrel: When a dog has a dam and sire from different breeds, also known as a crossbreed.

Chapter Twelve: Common Terms

Monorchid: A dog that only has one testicle.

Muzzle: The protruding section of the dog's head which includes the mouth, and nose.

Natural Breed: A breed of dog that developed without human interference.

Nesting Behavior: Seen in pregnant female dogs or those going through a false pregnancy, it is when the bitch prepares a place to whelp her young.

Neuter: When the dog's testicles are removed.

Nick: Refers to a breeding between two dogs that produces puppies that are desirable to the breed standard.

Nictitating Membrane: The third eyelid found in dogs.

Odd-Eyed: When one eye is a different color than the other.

Omnivore: An animal that eats both animal flesh and vegetation.

On-Dog Identification: Any form of identification that enables people to identify the dog.

Outcrossing: Breeding two dogs that are not related but are still of the same breed.

Overage Dam: An older dam that is older than 12 years old when she is bred.

Overage Sire: An older sire that is older than 12 years old when he is bred.

Overhang: A dog with an overly pronounced brow.

Chapter Twelve: Common Terms

Overshot: When the upper jaw protrudes out and the lower jaw is behind the upper jaw when the mouth is closed.

Ovulate: When the ovary releases a mature ovum.

Pants: Fur on the upper thighs that is longer and fringe like, also known as breeches, culottes and trousers.

Pack: Multiple dogs that live together.

Pedigree: A record of a dog's genealogy.

Pen Breeding: When a breeding occurs due to a male and female dog being penned together. The breeding is not witnessed.

Pile: The dense and soft hair that is the undercoat.

Pinking Up: Used to describe the nipples of a pregnant female dog when they begin to turn pink during a pregnancy.

Chapter Twelve: Common Terms

Plucking: The act of pulling out loose hair by hand.

Puppy Mill: A kennel that keeps dogs in unclean, crowded and inhumane conditions to continuously breed and sell the puppies. Do not purchase from puppy mills.

Purebred: A dog that has parents, grandparents and so on of the same breed.

Quick: The vein that is found in the dog's nail.

Registration Papers: Documents that show proof of breed and whether the dog is purebred.

Scent: The odor that is left in the air or on the ground by an animal.

Scissors Bite: When the lower incisors touch the upper incisors when the dog's mouth is closed.

Season: Refers to the period of time when the female dog can be bred.

Secondary Coat: The hairs that are found in the undercoat.

Selective Breeding: When a breeder chooses to breed two dogs together in the hopes of eliminating or achieving a trait.

Septum: The line that is seen between the two nostrils of the dog.

Service Dog: A specially trained dog that works with people who have disabilities.

Show Quality: A dog that is an excellent representation of the breed standard.

Chapter Twelve: Common Terms

Silent Heat: When a female dog goes into heat but shows no to little outward signs that she is in heat.

Single Coat: A dog that does not have an undercoat.

Sire: The male dog, specifically the male parent.

Smooth Coat: A coat that lies close to the body.

Soundness: A dog that has both optimal mental and physical health.

Spay: A procedure where the reproductive organs of a female are removed. This prevents heat and the female from getting pregnant.

Spectacles: When there are dark markings around the eyes.

Spread Hock: Refers to legs where the hock turns outward, which makes the paws turn inward, also known as barrel hocks.

Stacking: The way a dog stands when being exhibited in a dog show.

Standing Heat: The period during heat when the female will accept a male and can become pregnant.

Stray Dog: A dog that is homeless.

Teat: The nipple of an animal.

Topcoat: The hair that is stiffer and longer than the other hair. Usually protects the dog from the terrain and weather.

Trousers: Fur on the upper thighs that is longer and fringe like, also known as pants, culottes and breeches.

Chapter Twelve: Common Terms

Tuck Up: The waist of the dog where the body is shallower in depth.

Typey: A dog that conforms to the breed standard.

Underage Dam: A female dog that is bred before she is 8 months of age.

Underage Sire: A male dog that is bred before he is 7 months of age.

Undershot: When the lower jaw protrudes past the upper jaw when the mouth is closed.

Unsound: Refers to a dog that does not perform in the way it was bred for.

Vaccine: A shot that is given to a dog to help produce immunity to a specific disease.

Variety: When one breed has several subtypes, such as long haired and short haired, but both subtypes can be interbred.

Vent: The anus or anal opening.

Wean: The process of switching a puppy from milk to solid foods.

Weedy: A dog that lacks the musculature that is described in the standard.

Whelp Date: The date when the litter is born.

Whelping: This is the term used to describe a dam giving birth.

Withers: The shoulders of the dog.

Chapter Twelve: Common Terms

Zoonosis: A disease that can be passed from animal to human.

Chapter 13: Resources

Chapter Thirteen: Resources

Now that you know everything you can about the Alaskan Klee Kai, I want to leave you with resources that will help make owning your Alaskan Klee Kai easier. These are both specific breed resources for the Alaskan Klee Kai and general dog resources.

1. Alaskan Klee Kai Resources

The first resources that you should have on hand are those related directly to your Alaskan Klee Kai. Some excellent ones to start with are:

Alaskan Klee Kai Association of America: http://www.akkaoa.com/

Alaskan Klee Kai Rescue: http://www.akkrescue.com/

American Rare Breed Association: http://www.arba.org/

2. Alaskan Klee Kai Breeders

Since the breed is still being established, it can be difficult to find an Alaskan Klee Kai. I have started you off with a list of known Alaskan Klee Kai breeders.

Please bear in mind that I do not endorse any of the breeders and I urge you to read the chapter on finding an

Chapter Thirteen: Resources

Alaskan Klee Kai so you can learn how to find a reputable breeder.

AKLOKUM: https://www.facebook.com/KleeKaiAklokum

AKK's of Kabo: http://www.akksofkabo.com/

ALAKKAWA Kennels: http://www.alakkawa.com/

Alaskan Klee Kai Crookhill (Scotland):

http://www.akkc.co.uk

Alaskan Klee Kai Kennelette:

http://www.alaskankleekai.com/

Alaskan Klee Kai of Puget Sound: http://akkops.com/

Alaskan Klee Kai of Utah:

http://www.utahakk.com/Utah_Akk/Home.html

Alaskan Klee Kai - Norway: http://alaskankleekai.no/

Alberta Klee Kai: http://www.albertakleekai.com/

Aliak Kennels: http://www.aliakkennels.com/

Alikai AKK: http://www.alikaiakk.com/

Allerian Kennels: http://www.alleriankennels.com/

Alyeska Alaskan Klee Kai:

http://www.freewebs.com/akkalyeska/

Andalanes AKK: http://www.angelfire.com/al4/andalanes/

Angels' Crest Alaskan Klee Kai:

http://www.angelscrestkleekai.com/

Barkor's Alaskan Klee Kai: http://www.barkorakk.com/

BB Cook's Huggable Huskies:

http://www.huggablehuskies.com/

Chapter Thirteen: Resources

Clapham Klee Kai: http://claphamkleekai.tumblr.com/

Cocal Klee Kai: https://www.facebook.com/pages/Cocal-Klee-Kai/

Del Mar Klee Kai: http://www.delmarkleekai.com/

Fusion of XXcellence AKK: http://www.foxxakk.com/

Haakens AKK: http://www.haakensakk.webs.com/

Halfpint Huskies: http://www.halfpinthuskies.com/

Heart of Texas: http://www.kleekai.us/

Helerberg Huskies: http://www.helderberg-huskies.com/

HOPE Howllelujah Klee Kai:

http://www.howllelujahkleekai.com/

J.E.T.'s First Class Alaskan Klee Kai:

http://www.akktails.com/

Kenai Ridge Kennels:

http://kenairidge.wix.com/kenai-ridge-page

Kika's Klee Kai: http://www.kikaskleekai.com/

Klee Can: http://www.kleecan.com/

Klee Kai Magic: http://www.kleekaimagic.com/

Lee's Summit Alaskan Klee Kai:

http://www.kansascityhusky.com/

Mak's Pack: http://makspack.homestead.com/

MIKKA: http://akkadventure.com/

Naitok Kennels: http://www.minihusky.com/

Nordic Mini Huskies: http://www.nordicminihuskys.com/

Rocky Mountain Klee Kai: http://www.toyhusky.com/

Royal Star Estates: http://royalstarestates.webs.com/

Chapter Thirteen: Resources

Settle's Alaskan Klee Kai: http://www.youralaskankleekai.com/

Shalimar Acres: http://shalimaracres.wordpress.com/

Show-Me AKK: http://showmeakk.webs.com/

Sibridges' AKK: http://www.sibridgesalaskankleekai.webs.com/

Skyline AKK: http://www.freewebs.com/skylineakk/

Southpack Kennels: http://www.southpackkennels.com/

Steel City Klee Kai: http://www.steelcitykleekai.com/

Suska Kennel: http://www.freewebs.com/suskasakk/

Tesoro Creek Kennels: http://www.tesoroakk.com/

Tikanni Alaskan Klee Kai: http://tikaaniakk.webs.com/

T.O.P.A.Z. Alaskan Klee Kai: http://topazkleekai.ca/

TotemHill AKK: http://www.freewebs.com/jaguar1457/

Utah's Own AKK Kennel: http://utahsownkleekai.webs.com/

Wiebelhusky's Alaskan Klee Kai: http://www.wiebelhuskyskleekai.com/

World of Wonder: http://www.wowakk.com/faq.htm

Yakitat Kennels: http://www.yakitatkennelette.com/

2. Kennel Clubs

When it comes to dogs, kennel clubs are an important part of the dog world. A vast majority of countries have kennel clubs for purebred dogs and while the Alaskan Klee Kai is not accepted by many at this time, efforts are being made

Chapter Thirteen: Resources

to create a standard for the breed and have them accepted by various kennel clubs.

American Kennel Club: http://www.akc.org/

Australian National Kennel Council: http://www.ankc.org.au/

Canadian Kennel Club: http://www.ckc.ca/en

Danish Kennel Club: http://www.dkk.dk/

Estonian Kennel Union: http://kennelliit.ee/en/

Fédération Cynologue Internationale FCI: http://www.fci.be/

Finnish Kennel Club: http://www.kennelliitto.fi/

French Kennel Club: http://lifestream.aol.com/

German Kennel Club: http://www.vdh.de/home/

Italian Kennel Club: http://www.cta.it/

Irish Kennel Club: http://www.ikc.ie/

Japan Kennel Club: http://www.jkc.or.jp/

New Zealand Kennel Club: http://www.nzkc.org.nz/

Norwegian Kennel Club: http://www.nkk.no/

Swedish Kennel Club: http://www.skk.se/

Swiss Kennel Club: http://www.skg.ch/cms/home.html

United Kennel Club: http://www.ukcdogs.com/

3. Dog Owner Resources

Finally, here are a few dog owner resources that will help you navigate your way through pet ownership. It is important to note that I am not affiliated with any of these

Chapter Thirteen: Resources

sites and it is important to discuss your dog's health and well being with your vet and other trained professionals.

AltVetMed: http://www.altvetmed.org/

American College of Veterinary Nutrition: http://www.acvn.org/

American Dog Trainers Network: http://www.inch.com/~dogs/

Best Friends: http://bestfriends.org/

Breeder.net: http://www.breeders.net/

Canine Eye Registration Foundation: http://web.vmdb.org/home/CERF.aspx

Canine Health Foundation: http://www.akcchf.org/

Canine Health Information Center: http://www.caninehealthinfo.org/

Dog Owners' Guide: http://www.canismajor.com/

Dog Time: http://dogtime.com/

Dr. Foster and Smith Pet Education: http://www.peteducation.com/

Healthy Pet: http://www.aaha.org/pet_owner/

Medline Plus: http://www.nlm.nih.gov/medlineplus/pethealth.html

Orthopedic Foundation for Animals: http://www.offa.org/

PAW: http://www.paw-rescue.org/

Chapter Thirteen: Resources

Pet Diets: https://www.petdiets.com/

Pet Pharmacy: http://www.veterinarypartner.com

Petstyle: http://www.petstyle.com/

Terrific Pets: http://www.terrificpets.com/

VetInfo: http://www.vetinfo.com/

Vetmedicine: http://vetmedicine.about.com/

Vetquest: http://www.vetquest.com/

Whole Pet: http://www.wholepetvet.com/

4. Photo Credits

The photos within this book have kindly been donated by:

Cover Photo – Pamela Renfrew
Chapter 1 – Hot Shots Tubes (Lisa Chapman)
Chapter 2 – Hot Shots Tubes (Lisa Chapman), Pamela Renfrew (Page 16)
Chapter 3 – Hot Shots Tubes (Lisa Chapman)
Chapter 4 – Hot Shots Tubes (Lisa Chapman)
Chapter 5 – Hot Shots Tubes (Lisa Chapman), Pamela Renfrew Page 35, 41)
Chapter 6 – Hot Shots Tubes (Lisa Chapman), Barbara Manley (Page 47), Pamela Renfrew (Page 51, 56)
Chapter 7 – Hot Shots Tubes (Lisa Chapman), Pamela Renfrew (Page 68)
Chapter 8 – Hot Shots Tubes (Lisa Chapman), Pamela Renfrew (Page 82)
Chapter 9 – Hot Shots Tubes (Lisa Chapman)
Chapter 10 – Hot Shots Tubes (Lisa Chapman)
Chapter 11 – Hot Shots Tubes (Lisa Chapman), Pamela Renfrew (Page 143)
Chapter 12 – Hot Shots Tubes (Lisa Chapman)
Chapter 13 – Hot Shots Tubes (Lisa Chapman)

www.ingramcontent.com/pod-product-compliance
Lightning Source LLC
Chambersburg PA
CBHW030436010526
44118CB00011B/663